Counselling and Supporting
Children in Distress

Counselling and Supporting Children in Distress

Sonia Sharp and Helen Cowie

SAGE Publications
London • Thousand Oaks • New Delhi

First published 1998

SAGE Publications Ltd
6 Bonhill Street
London EC2A 4PU

SAGE Publications Inc
2455 Teller Road
Thousand Oaks, California 91320

SAGE Publications India Pvt Ltd
32, M-Block Market
Greater Kailash – I
New Delhi 110 048

British Library Cataloguing in Publication data

A catalogue record for this book is
available from the British Library

ISBN 0 7619 5618 2
ISBN 0 7619 5619 0 (pbk)

Library of Congress catalog card number 98–61236

Typeset by Photoprint, Torquay, Devon.
Printed in Great Britain by Biddles Ltd, Guildford, Surrey

CONTENTS

ACKNOWLEDGEMENTS

The authors would like to thank the following people for their contributions to the writing of this book: Jo Barnard, Ginny Farmiloe, Michael Hayes, Ian Rivers, Peter K. Smith, Paul Naylor and Gill Taylor.

1

THE DEVELOPING CHILD: NEEDS AND RIGHTS

'I can't imagine not being frightened.'

'I don't think I can go on any more.'

'I would like to end it all.'

'Suicide would be better than going to school again.'

(Children's words quoted in MacLeod and Morris, 1996,
pp. 1–2)

The rationale: meeting needs and promoting rights

Most adults would be shocked if they thought that a child in their care felt so desperately about life that they turned to an anonymous help line to be heard. Yet such statements are heard every day and night by ChildLine telephone counsellors. What leads children to make such statements as those quoted above and how can we as adults improve our systems for giving children the support they need in these circumstances?

It is estimated that 2 million children in the UK have some form of mental health problem, including eating disorders, anxiety, depression. There is a rising level of suicide, and emotional and conduct disorders are found in 10 per cent of children and 20 per cent of adolescents:

> About two in one hundred children under the age of twelve are depressed to the extent that they would benefit from seeing a specialist Child Psychiatrist. However, four in five in every one hundred of this age show significant distress and some of these could be described as on the edge of depression. The rate goes up with age, so that about five teenagers in one hundred are seriously depressed, and at least twice that number show significant distress. These figures apply to stable settled populations in reasonably good social circumstances. In troubled, inner-city areas with high rates of broken homes, poor

community support and raised neighbourhood crime rates, the level of depression may be twice the figures we have quoted.

These figures relating to depression mean that in a secondary school in a reasonably settled area, with one thousand children on the roll, about 50 children will be depressed in any one year. In a primary school with about 400 children on the roll in an inner-city area, about eight children will be seriously depressed, and double that number will be significantly distressed. Other children in these schools, and often quite a lot of them, will have problems such as disruptive behaviour and learning difficulties. (Mental Health Foundation, 1993)

What these figures tell us is that the majority of children and adolescents appear to deal with the difficulties they encounter in the course of growing up. They may be sad, angry or disappointed, but they are not overwhelmed by the ups and downs of life. Wilson (1996, p. 19) argues: 'children in "good enough" mental health are able, in fact, to learn from their difficulties and make the most of their abilities'. However, there are significant numbers of children and adolescents who do find it difficult to deal with the vicissitudes of their lives. Their mental health problems may be mild and short-lived (for example, the emotional reaction to moving from one neighbourhood to another) or more serious and longer-term (for example, the emotional response to the death of a parent, or the impact on self-esteem of being bullied by peers over time).

This book is about the ways in which adults can play an active part in helping young people whom they know to be in emotional distress. There are times, of course, when specialist intervention, for example by an educational psychologist or a counsellor, is essential. The British Association for Counselling (BAC) clarifies the professional role: 'People become engaged in counselling when a person, occupying regularly or temporarily the role of counsellor, offers and agrees explicitly to give time, attention and respect to another person, or persons, who will be temporarily in the role of client' (1995). But increasingly we need to recognize the value of sensitive listening and attending on the part of a parent, friend or teacher to a child in need. Even when the child is in the care of professionals, there will always be the need for a complementary contribution by other adults in the child's circle.

Children's needs

Children have certain needs. If they are not met, then normal social, emotional and cognitive developmental processes are put at risk. Summaries of children's needs (for example, Adcock and

White, 1985; Coleman and Warren-Adamson, 1992; Dalrymple and Hough, 1995) describe the following aspects.

- **Basic physical care**: children need to be assured of warmth, shelter, food and rest; they need to be kept clean.
- **Protection**: they need to be kept safe and to be protected from danger, including the risk of sexual abuse or physical violence.
- **Security, guidance, support and control**: children need to have a sense of continuity of care and the expectation that the family unit will remain stable. Routines and predictable patterns of care, reasonable sets of rules and consistent monitoring facilitate this sense of security. They need to be in a context where there is consistent, firm guidance on acceptable social behaviour, and where adults act as 'good-enough' role models.
- **Love, affection and respect**: children need to have affectionate, respectful physical contact, to be comforted when in distress, to be held with tenderness; to be listened to; to be taken seriously; to be given opportunities for challenge, exploration and the growth of a sense of competence; to be encouraged to share feelings, including those that express anger, bewilderment and hurt.
- **Stimulation to learn and access to schooling**: throughout the pre-school years, children need to explore their world at their own pace; to have stimulating materials, playthings and books; their questions need to be answered. Once at school, they need to have access to appropriate educational opportunities in contexts where there is a concern to provide them with resources to help them learn and realize their potential.
- **Autonomy and responsibility**: children and young people need to gain the experience of taking responsibility for themselves and others in age-appropriate ways, for example, by tidying away toys, helping with household chores, managing their pocket money. They need to be given helpful information, for example on sexual matters, to help them to make informed, reasoned decisions which affect themselves, their families and friends. This information should not be weighted with value-laden judgements. There should be opportunities to deal with ethical dilemmas and interpersonal conflicts and to live with the consequences, whatever these may be.

Children's rights

Unfortunately, it is not enough to identify children's developmental *needs*. Increasingly society has an obligation to establish a basic set of children's *rights* which it is unacceptable, or even illegal, to contravene. This in itself is often contentious. For example, adults find it hard to agree on the extent to which they should be prepared to share power with children in suitable ways which both ensure the safety of the child and enable the child to learn how to make decisions – even take decisions which may be mistaken. To help clarify some of these debates we first consider some aspects of the impact of the Children Act (HMSO, 1989) in the UK and, next, the United Nations Convention on the Rights of the Child (United Nations, 1991).

The Children Act states that the child's welfare must be paramount and that adults must ascertain what the wishes and feelings of the child are; in legal cases, courts should take into account the emotional needs of the child. The Children Act requires all local authority agencies to work together in the best interests of protecting the child. This means, among other things, that teachers are legally obliged to share their knowledge of abuse or significant harm to the child with other agencies, most frequently social services.

The Children Act shifts the emphasis from parents' rights *over* their children to their responsibilities *towards* the young people in their care. For example, when parents divorce, the local authorities have a duty to protect and promote the welfare of the children involved; similarly, the courts must now pay due attention to the wishes of the child. A process of conciliation is now more common because of the Children Act, in line with its intention to benefit children in this situation. At the same time, in practice courts have the right to judge the child's competence to make autonomous decisions and may, as a result, disregard children's wishes in the wider context of 'the best interests of the child'. It is extremely difficult to achieve a balance between what the child thinks he or she wants at the time and what, in the view of adults, may be best for the child in the longer term. And who is right – the adult or the child?

In a wider arena, the United Nations Convention on the Rights of the Child (United Nations, 1991) proposes an international perspective on the rights of children to *life itself* and to a reasonable *quality of life*. This document gives nations the opportunity to define human rights standards for children, to identify gaps in the provision for those rights, and to set this in the context of an international binding agreement. The 54 Articles in the Convention cover a range of children's rights which have been categorized (Children's Rights Development Unit [CRDU], 1993, p. 6) as:

- **protection**: from abuse, torture and armed conflict;
- **provision**: of the right to life, state care, education, health services and social security;
- **participation**: in decision-making on matters affecting the child, with due consideration for the age and maturity of the child; in judicial and administrative proceedings affecting the child, either directly or through a representative.

By emphasizing non-discrimination, acting in the best interests of the child, and listening to the views of the child, the UN Convention built on earlier legislation by specifying not only children's rights to protection from physical and mental violence, and provision of certain medical, educational and social services, but also their rights to participation – so recommending some political voice for children.

Some frameworks have been developed in schools to facilitate the process of democratic participation within school contexts while at the same time creating a balance between the rights of the individual child on the one hand and the constraints inherent in operating in a community on the other. The Elton Report (DES, 1989), for example, advised that schools create environments where the quality of relationships and a sense of responsibility are valued. It was recommended that teachers should listen to pupils and incorporate their opinions into school policies, especially those concerned with behaviour and school ethos in a context where pupils and teachers might begin to develop a process of negotiation of responsibilities and rights on both sides. Difficult decisions (for example, with regard to the exclusion of certain pupils) have to be made in situations where disturbing children challenge school policies and pose a threat to the rights of teachers and other pupils.

More recent legislation (DFE, 1992) states that children should be educated for active citizenship. The balance, argued the authors of this paper, is to be between rights and expectations on the one hand and responsibilities on the other. Schools should be active in providing a moral code which includes a concern for others, self-respect and basic values of truth and honesty.

However, very little has been done in the UK to facilitate the process of greater participation on the part of children in the decisions which affect their lives. For many, childhood continues to be characterized by 'low status, little power and almost no control over the outcomes of their lives' (Children's Rights Development Unit [CRDU], 1994, p. xiv). At present, children have no rights in law either to be consulted or to be taken into account on any matter concerning their individual rights within the educational system. Nor is there any formal requirement to hear the views of an individual child concerning any issue relating to their education, for example religion or sex education, or problems in school such as bullying and harassment (Dalrymple and Hough, 1995, p. 78).

The recommendations of the UN Convention are, in practice, difficult to achieve. Many teachers underestimate the potential of children to play a part in promoting positive values and a caring ethos in the peer group. Many adults ignore the fact that the process of being involved in decision-making for change can be as valuable to the individuals involved as the outcomes. Much educational practice continues to ignore children's basic democratic rights (Lloyd, 1997) and, in fact, there remains no requirement on schools to implement the recommendations of the UN Convention at all.

There are cultural and social influences on the ways in which we think both about children and the impact which psychologists and other social scientists have on policies to ensure that children the world over are given at least basic provision for their needs. The potential mismatch between the child's developmental needs and the realities of his or her social situation are difficult to resolve, and attempts to safeguard children's basic rights worldwide demonstrate the ambivalence which all societies appear to have towards the children in their care (Burman, 1996). Hojat (1997) comments that, despite the widespread dissemination of literature on the United Nations Convention on the Rights of the Child, very few psychologists and professionals in mental health services in the USA actively promote its tenets. A similar situation exists in the UK (Lloyd, 1997).

In order to unravel some of the factors involved, we take a closer look at the interaction between family patterns of relationships and the wider context of the culture within which these family members exist.

Relationships within the family

The UN Convention states in its preamble: 'the family, as the fundamental group in society and the natural environment for the growth and well-being of all its members and particularly children, should be afforded the necessary protection and assistance so that it can fully assume its responsibilities within the community' (1991).

A large body of research (for example, Bretherton, 1990; Dunn, 1988) confirms that experiences within the family play a key role in influencing the child's capacity to form and maintain relationships within the family, to anticipate social interaction in the context of the wider community and to have firmly established strategies for forming new relationships outside the family. Attachment theory offers one important perspective. Bowlby (1969) proposed that from a very early age children develop internal working models of self in relation to others based on their relationships with primary caregivers, usually the parents or other members of the family. It was his view that these cognitive structures which represented the daily interactions with significant people in the child's life would persist into adult life, and that their origins lay in the sensitivity with which the primary caregivers had responded to the child's needs and the quality of these caregivers' responses to the child's distress when it occurred. This perspective is particularly relevant to core aspects of children's responses to separation and loss, and we will return to it in Chapter 3: Children and Grief.

Secure attachment relationships in the family, from this perspective, facilitate the development of well-organized and flexible internal representations of self in relation to others, and foster the sense 'of the world as a reasonably trustworthy place' (Bretherton, 1996). Securely attached infants have an internal working model of caregivers who are available and responsive. Children who have experienced relationships as warm and loving are more likely to see themselves as likeable and to expect others to see them in that way. Resnick (1993) argues that the secure child is emotionally strong enough to explore the environment yet still maintain contact with the attachment figure and 'check back' regularly for comfort and support. In this way, the child increasingly engages with others in his or her environment and so cognitive and social development is enhanced. Secure children are, in a sense, 'attuned' to their social environment and learn how to respond differentially to people they know and those who are unfamiliar. With their friends, they can seek out comfort when they are apart from their primary attachment figures.

Insecure attachment relationships in the family, by contrast, do not build that sense of trust; as a result, the child acquires a different internal working model. Insecure-avoidant children are more likely to dismiss the importance of relationships during times of stress and try to rely on their own resources (Crittenden, 1992), whereas insecure-ambivalent children are so preoccupied with the attachment figure that they find it difficult to engage with other people and to explore their environment in a productive way.

Sadly, children like Lloyd (case study follows) whose experiences within the family have been harsh and rejecting, and who have not been comforted when in distress, are likely to have low expectations of relationships and to act in such a way as to elicit rejection, dislike or avoidance in others (Goleman, 1996). As a result, they are likely to miss essential opportunities to enhance relationships with peers and adults outside the family. The lack of attunement between Lloyd and his parents has been reflected in many subsequent relationships with teachers and peers. Yet there are ways in which other relationships might 'repair' the damage. Support for the parents from a counsellor (in improving their unhappy marriage) or from a health professional or educational social worker (in working on their parenting skills, including Lloyd's personal hygiene) might change the way in which they relate to Lloyd and encourage them to provide better physical and emotional care for him. At school he could be offered specialist help with his learning difficulties. A buddying system (see Chapter 5) could offer peer support; the educational psychologist could establish a 'circle of friends' (Chapter 5) to create an opportunity for the peer group to work constructively with him in order to facilitate better relationships and tackle his quarrelsome behaviour. His teacher could try to integrate Lloyd into cooperative group work activities instead of isolating him in response to his disruptive behaviour. She could ensure that he is given tasks which are appropriately matched to his educational needs and in which he is successful. She could also take time to praise him on the occasions, however rare, when he is acting pro-socially in the classroom and at break time. Over time, if some of these interventions were put in place, it is likely that Lloyd's low expectations of relationships would change and his self-esteem grow.

Case study of an insecurely attached child

Lloyd, aged 8, is small in stature and very unhappy at school because, in his words, he is 'always being bullied'. Lloyd does not always have clean clothes to wear and other children laugh at him for being smelly and unkempt. His mum complains to Lloyd that he was 'a difficult, fretful baby and has not improved since'. He is often late in the mornings and regularly goes out to school without any breakfast. For as long as he can remember, his parents have quarrelled and argued. His father often threatens to leave home and Lloyd is afraid that one day he will leave for good.

At school he cannot always concentrate, so his teacher, Mrs Mayes, gets impatient with him for making mistakes in class work. She also notes how difficult it is for him to work in groups. His behaviour is so disruptive, she says, that often she has to ask him to work on his own. In her words, 'He sparks things off for the others. He picks on other children's weaknesses and says nasty things about them. They do not want to work with him. This situation is repeated when children choose partners for an activity. He is never chosen so I have to pair him off with someone else. That person will usually complain loudly about having to work with Lloyd.' The other children say that he is the one who is always picking fights with them. A typical comment is: 'Lloyd thumps me on the back when we're working. He thumps me so I thump him back.' Classmates agree that he is excessively quarrelsome and easy to annoy.

Lloyd cannot think of anything positive to say about the others in his class. He complains, for example, about all the fighting that is always going on. He says that it is not fair that he is 'often told off by Mrs Mayes for picking on other children'. Lloyd is of the opinion that no one likes him. He wishes that, 'all the bad people left and friendly people came back into school'.

Lloyd's case illustrates the view, supported by a large body of research, that insecurely attached children are often those whose caregivers for whatever reason have not been able to give them the support and love which they need. These children's model of relationships is one in which caregivers are not available, are unpredictable, or are cold and rejecting. The lack of attunement can have devastating effects on the child unless other relationships can repair the damage.

Consistencies across time are reported in the research literature to support the view that the quality of the attachments developed in the early years predicts to later relationships. For example, research by Cassidy (1988) and Main and Cassidy (1988), using the Adult Attachment Interview, provides retrospective evidence that the patterns established in infancy can endure right through to adulthood. Work by Erickson et al. (1985) has shown that the quality of attachments at the age of 12 months, using the Strange Situation as a measure, can predict to teacher ratings of the child, the extent of behaviour problems and the quality of peer relationships during the first school years. Wright et al. (1995) used the Separation Anxiety Test to compare the responses of 8 to 12-year-olds having clinical treatment for behaviour disturbance and a normal control group of the same age. Securely attached children in this sample tended to acknowledge the anxiety caused by separation from caregivers but also demonstrated a reasonable coping strategy. For example, one child said he would feel a bit scared if left alone but that he would 'try and have some fun' and 'imagine that mum and dad are in the house'. Insecurely attached children were more likely to deny their anxiety or to give inappropriate coping strategies. One child said, 'So he sets booby traps and ends up hitting mum in the face with iron bars and blow torches. So he sits and watches TV but he gets burnt by the fire and goes to hospital; his mum visits him and he's dead.'

Weiss (1991) also proposes that there is a continuity – from childhood, through adolescence to adulthood – in the characteristics of attachment behaviour, particularly in the arousal associated with attachment and in the energy with which individuals respond when there is a threat to the attachment bond. Usually, he argues, the process of relinquishing parents as attachment figures does not begin until early adolescence when young people develop a concept of their parents as people they love and are bonded to, and to whom they feel obligation, but also ceasing to conceive of them not as people who will always guarantee security. Adolescents are likely to begin the process of actively *not* needing their parents to meet their emotional needs and may turn instead to peers to find security and a sense of well-being. However, loss of a close relationship in adolescence still produces responses of distress, such as calling for the loved one, crying, searching, repeatedly and restlessly recalling the image of the attachment figure and experiencing helplessness, fear and despair. Those who are not successful in finding members of the peer group with whom to bond may be lonely much of the time. 'Studies of loneliness suggest that it is in the developmental phase from late adolescence to early adulthood that loneliness occurs most frequently and, when it does occur, is most painful' (Weiss, 1991, p. 71–2).

The family in a cultural context

We can say with some confidence the early years lay a strong foundation for later emotional development and many of the difficulties experienced by children later on can be traced back to the first relationships with primary caregivers. At the same time, we must be aware of the wide range of ways in which the attachment relationship can be expressed depending on the values and customs of the cultural group to which the child belongs. Secure and insecure patterns of attachment have universal characteristics which cross all boundaries of social class, community and culture; however, parents of differing cultures value the infant's security for different reasons and elaborate their behaviour towards the child into culturally specific forms. Takahashi (1990) argues that the Strange Situation must be interpreted carefully when used across cultures. Japanese infants, for example, are extremely distressed when left alone in the Strange Situation experiment, but such a response can be explained because children of this age are never left by themselves by Japanese families.

In order more fully to understand the dynamics of family relationships across cultures we need to be sensitive to norms and rules which are 'part of a larger web of cultural meanings regarding conceptions of self and other' (Harwood et al., 1995, p. 141), and take account of the interplay between experience of self and understanding of behaviour of others, with the internal working model of relationships acting as mediator between self and culture. The Anglo-American mothers in the study by Harwood et al. (1995) favoured independence and autonomy in their children, whereas Puerto Rican mothers encouraged 'proper demeanour' – respect for adults, calmness and politeness.

There are wide differences in cultural practices relating to the expression of feelings by males and females, for example in the application of rules over whether it is appropriate to express certain emotions. The expression of anger is socialized differently for boys and girls, depending on the ways in which the culture construes gender role expectations:

> In many Western cultures young boys, though more harshly reprimanded than girls for non-compliance, are also subtly encouraged to display less inhibited, fiercer behaviour. Older girls who commit anti-

social or delinquent acts, conversely, have been found to receive harsher punishments. (Barrett and Jones, 1997, p. 17)

Studies of family background factors in the development of resiliency indicate a broad range of ways in which families in different cultures or social groups reward qualities such as risk taking and independence, or encourage the young people in their care to believe that personal effort will lead to success in the face of adversity (therefore stimulating internal locus of control) (Werner, 1989). Kimchi and Schaffner (1990) report a study carried out by Block and Gjerde (1986). They found that resilient girls tended to come from households which did not overprotect but still provided good emotional support and which encouraged risk taking and independence. Resilient boys, however, experienced family backgrounds which provided greater structure, rules, supervision and emotional expressiveness. These findings suggest that parents and caretakers may need to develop different approaches to nurturing and management for children according to gender.

Schulman (1993) measured attachments to parents, close friends and coping behaviours of 121 12- and 13-year-olds. He found that active coping was related to attachment to parents rather than peers for boys. Passivity was linked to rejection by parents and lack of emotional support. Boys generally preferred to use their own internal resources to resolve problems, whereas girls relied on both parental and peer support systems. Schulman also noted that in contexts where peer groups require conformity and do not show respect for autonomy, there is less adaptive coping especially among boys.

Seiffge-Krenke (1993) reported a study she carried out into coping among adolescents who were chronically ill. She found that children who coped well with their illness came from families whose members were cohesive, demonstrated a high degree of organization and control but discouraged autonomy. Although the youngsters coped well with their illness they showed poor autonomy outside the family, experiencing problems separating from their parents, establishing social networks or developing close friendships. Autonomy in family relationships seems to be a significant feature in the development of resilience and possibly the development of social relationships outside the home. These findings raise some questions: is it really over-cohesiveness in families *per se* that contributes to poor social relationships or is it that over-cohesiveness discourages autonomy? What is the overlap between autonomy, perceived personal control and competency beliefs?

Viewing relationships in a wider social context, Bronfenbrenner (1979) proposes the model of a system within a system. From this perspective, it is not only the family which influences the emotional and social growth of the child, but also the environmental setting in which the child in the family exists. Bronfenbrenner suggests a series of 'ecosystems': the 'microsystem' of, for example, the family with its particular history and patterns of relationships; the 'mesosystem', including the range of systems with which the child has direct contact; the 'exosystem', including those systems with which the child has only indirect contact, for example, the parents' workplace; and the 'macrosystem', the wider social context of the society or culture within which

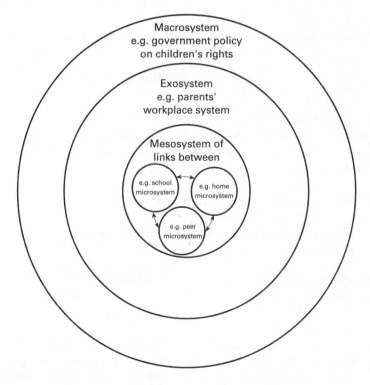

Figure 1.1   *Adapted from Bronfenbrenner's ecological model*

the family happens to exist. Fuller discussion of the model is found in Bronfenbrenner and Ceci (1994).

As you can see from Figure 1.1, the development of the child can be influenced by events in any one of the systems. In fact, Bronfenbrenner proposes that human development is deeply affected by the process of coming to understand and restructure increasingly complex systems. He argues that in the absence of good support systems, external stresses can put unbearable pressures on even the strongest families. Where families are less functional, there is a greater risk to the young 'because of the erosion of countless small nourishing exchanges between parent and child that build emotional competencies' (Bronfenbrenner, 1994, quoted in Goleman, 1996, p. 234). Goleman (1996, p. 234) takes a pessimistic view of contemporary 'financially besieged families, where parents work long hours, children are left too often to their own devices, where day care is too often inadequate.'

Social context as a protective factor

Social context is an important protective or risk factor. Family background factors such as parenting style and parent–child relationships influence the skills and attitudes of the young person. Other environmental influences such as cultural style, socioeconomic status and religious belief have also been implicated (Felner et al., 1995). Pryor-Brown et al. (1986) found that children of unemployed parents experienced higher stress, demonstrated more socially inept behaviours and experienced greater peer rejection. Conger et al. (1994) identified that financial hardship within a family led to more arguments and conflicts between the parents, which in turn contributed to higher levels of stress among the children. Although socio-economic disadvantage is correlated with greater stress, studies of competence and resilience have shown that regardless of background children are generally resourceful. Competence is the mediating variable which predicts positive or negative outcomes (Garmezy and Masten, 1991).

Social support can be provided by the family, by peers or by other adults such as teachers and counsellors. Wetherington and Kessler (1991) note that not only is the actual availability of support protective but also the *belief* that others are available to provide emotional support. They found that people who believed that others would support them were more resistant to psychological distress. Compas (1987) found a direct link between social support and psychological outcomes of stressful situations. Ryan (1989) investigated social support at different stages in stressful events in 103 8- to 12-year-olds. Ryan found that children used social support *during* a stressful experience and avoidant strategies *after* a stressful experience. DuBois et al. (1992), however, compared levels of psychological distress following major events in students who had high or low support from friends, family and school personnel. In this study, students were followed up over a two-year period with measures of adaptation to major life events. They found no significant 'buffering effect' resulting from friend or family support but did for support from school personnel. Although social support has been widely accepted as an important mechanism in successful management of stress, Gore and Colton (1991) point out some crucial gender differences. They note that adolescent girls' self-esteem is more dependent on relationships with others. Furthermore, social support has greater importance as a coping device for females than a sense of personal competency. The opposite is more true for males.

Rutter (1998) has recently evaluated the outcomes for 165 children who had experienced terrible deprivation and neglect within Romanian orphanages but had been subsequently adopted by loving families in the UK. He found that in this nurturing environment they were able to make good progress and, even though on arrival more than half were described as experiencing significant learning difficulties, most had made age appropriate progress without any educational intervention or counselling. The special ingredient for success seems to have been the adoptive parents' love and attention.

The book

The aim of this book is to outline the ways in which all adults involved in the care of children and adolescents can play a part in supporting these young people at times of emotional distress. We argue throughout this is not the sole domain of the expert. We are all responsible for the emotional well-being of young people and, potentially, can play our part in alleviating their distress. Professional therapeutic work with children and young people must take place within a clear framework of knowledge, competence and ethics (Cowie and Pecherek, 1994). However, there are many ways in which any adult can help and support a young person in distress. Indeed, it can sometimes be unhelpful to the child to have contact with new and unfamiliar adults at the time of unhappiness since he or she is likely to turn first to significant figures; at such times, by relocating the supportive relationship to a professional, we can unwittingly undermine the quality and confidence of natural supportive relationships. In this book we discuss the roles to be played by parents, teachers and other adults in the child's life in creating an environment which is conducive to mental health (Wilson, 1996).

In Chapter 2 we look at the sources of unhappiness among young people, and explore the causes of stress. We examine the influence of adult–child dialogue in the construction of the child's representation of self and others as supportive or harmful. Everyday stressors are considered as well as the impact of critical incidents or traumas on current mental health and outlook on life. We examine the interaction between children's distress, adult responses to it and effective coping. We also look at the resilience which many children show, and discuss some of the ways in which adults can strengthen this natural capacity for coping and the factors which can buffer children from the worst impacts of stressful events in their lives.

In Chapter 3 we explore the issue of children's grief over serious loss. Every year over 10,000 young people aged from 10 to 18 years lose a parent and many thousands more lose a grandparent, sibling or close friend. Yet the services for helping young people to cope with bereavement are often inadequate. By considering the nature of loss and the processes of grieving as they apply to children and adolescents, we examine ways in which adults can work supportively with individual children.

In Chapter 4 we discuss creative approaches – including the use of art work, storytelling, drama and play – as media for children to express their emotions, explore and understand their experiences and work out future solutions. These kinds of approaches have traditionally been used within communities and families to make sense of everyday difficulties; the telling and retelling of events, re-enactments, drawings and folk songs feature in all cultures. Such approaches are also used widely in clinical settings as therapy and can be adapted for use in educational and family settings. We describe how the different forms of creative approach can be used as interventions to help young people deal with distressing or disturbing feelings.

In Chapter 5 we discuss the role of peers in alleviating young people's distress. Peer support systems can offer help when it is most needed. These systems appear in a variety of forms including befriending, Circles of Friends, mediation and conflict resolution, and counselling-based approaches. We overview how they work, how useful they are to young people in need, and their wider impact on the school's emotional climate. We evaluate the role of this type of intervention in facilitating a sense of responsibility in young people over the distress of their peers, and discuss some of the critical factors which must be taken into account when setting up a peer support service.

In Chapter 6 we explore the common fears and phobias of childhood and show how they change over time, how they may emerge in school settings, and how they can affect behaviour at home and in school. Practical guidance is offered on ways in which adults can work with young people to help them understand and overcome these anxieties, and to teach them effective coping strategies.

In Chapter 7 we consider the impact of social rejection and victimization on children's mental health, with a particular focus on documented interventions to improve social relationships and reduce bullying. We look at the social contexts in which bullying behaviour is likely to flourish and consider the role of the bystander in supporting or challenging antisocial behaviour. We consider the particular role of whole school policies in effecting change over the longer term.

In Chapter 8 we review the nature of aggressive and disruptive behaviour. We emphasize the need to understand why these behaviours occur and suggest that changes in the young person can often be achieved through changing the social environment. Again, as in Chapter 7, we explore the constructive use of cooperative group work to effect changes in values and behaviours. Traditional approaches to behaviour management are discussed as well as more recent innovations such as Family Conferencing (O'Connell, 1994).

In Chapter 9 we review the impact of programmes for emotional literacy and social competence. We end by affirming the importance with which all adults should view the task of supporting young people in need by creating contexts to promote mental health and emotional resilience.

2

STRESS AND DISTRESS: UNHAPPINESS IN CHILDHOOD AND ADOLESCENCE

DISTRESS: Anguish or affliction affecting the body, spirit or community; to subject to severe pain or pressure; to put to sore straits; to afflict or exhaust; to cause pain or anxiety to.

(*Shorter Oxford English Dictionary*, 1983, p. 582)

Unhappiness falls along a dual continuum of persistency and intensity. Children and young people can feel unhappy because their parents have told them they cannot have the new pair of trainers they have set their heart on, that they are expected home by a particular time, or that they can only watch TV or go out with friends after they have completed certain tasks. These sources of unhappiness are most probably short term and arise through parental monitoring and supervision which is part of appropriate care taking. Outside the home, unhappiness can result from the break-up of a friendship, playground teasing and bullying, achieving poor marks in a school assignment, and so on. Emotions are a part of human life and every day we experience a mixture of emotions such as anger, sadness and joy which result from one-off, short-term incidents and situations.

At the other end of the spectrum are long-term or major incidents which cast our usual daily lives into a maelstrom of intense emotional reaction and physiological response. Abuse, separation or neglect, death, illness and accident lie along this end of the continuum. Psychological researchers have investigated this continuum of unhappiness under the conceptual umbrella of 'stress', a term which originated from the word 'distress'. The field of stress research is broad and encompasses short-term unhappiness through to major trauma and long term impact. In this chapter we will focus on some of the key concepts of stress and coping in childhood and adolescence.

Defining stress

Definitions of stress have become increasingly sophisticated and interactional, acknowledging that individual differences and contextual factors lead to great variation in how different people respond to and manage the same stressor and how any individual's responses also vary temporally and situationally.

Lazarus and Abramovitz (1962) identified that the experience of stress was dependent on the person's interpretation, perception or appraisal of how significant a harmful, threatening and challenging event might be. The notion of individual difference in perception of, and response to, stress has become central to its study. The level of distress experienced by each child in any stressful situation will depend not only on the nature of the action but also on the young person's perceptions of its harmfulness. Cox (1978) proposed a transactional model of stress which was both complex and dynamic. Perception of an environmental, psychological or physical demand is followed by cognitive appraisal of the demand against ability to cope. If a 'critical imbalance' is perceived, then this leads to the emotional experience of stress and psychophysical changes. Coping strategies are implemented and the outcomes of these are fed back into the cognitive appraisal loop. Freeman (1986) describes stress as: 'some form of pressure or demand experienced by an individual which they perceive negatively and which might lead to emotional or psychological distress'. Freeman emphasizes the importance of coping as a psychological response to stress which is integral to our resolution of the situation.

Rice et al. (1993) propose a model of stress in childhood and adolescence which recognizes the interrelationship of the number of stressful events, the nature of stressful events and the synchronicity of different stressors with other important developmental events or processes (see Figure 2.1). These are mediated by social support and/or internal resources (self-esteem, coping responses, etc.). They describe stress as arising when there is insufficient 'goodness of fit' between the changes and challenges faced by the young person and the available support and individual coping resources which can be drawn upon in meeting these challenges or changes.

Stress is not just about an individual reaction to a single event or situation. It arises through the complex interaction of pressures

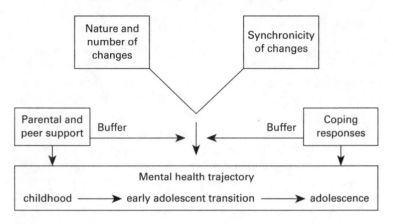

Figure 2.1   *Model of developmental transition from Rice et al.*
(1993)

and events – immediately and over time – and support systems and coping responses.

Studies of causes of stress in childhood and adolescence

Garmezy and Rutter (1983) categorized sources of stress into five main groupings:

- loss
- chronically disturbed relationships
- events that change the family status quo
- events which require social adaptation
- acute negative events such as trauma.

Compas (1987) asked 658 12- to 17-year-olds to list daily hassles and major life events which they had experienced over the previous six months. This generated 2705 major events and 4210 daily hassles. These were collapsed into logical groupings and used to form the basis of a life-event checklist of around 150 items. The items could be clustered into five content areas: school, family, friendship, personal health, appearance.

Sharp and Thompson (1992) surveyed 455 14- to 16-year-olds from three different schools. The most frequently experienced and most stressful events were:

- death of a close family member
- illness/injury of a close family member
- personal illness or injury
- poor relationship with a teacher
- arguments within the family
- having to attend uninteresting lessons
- arguing with friends
- exams
- being told off by a teacher/being in trouble in school
- difficulty with school work.

In a survey of 1482 10- to 15-year-olds in Western Australia, Garton and Pratt (1995) found that the most frequent stressors reported by adolescents were:

- having a hard day
- exam pressures
- poor relationships with the teacher
- being bored in lessons
- not being able to afford something they really want.

Silverman et al. (1995) interviewed 141 boys and 132 girls who were aged between 7 and 12 years and who attended school in Florida. They did not enquire about stress, rather about worries. The children were asked 'Do you worry about . . .?' and then presented with a particular theme. Two very interesting findings emerged. First, the things which worried the youngsters most seriously were the things they had least experience of: war, disasters, personal harm. The highest frequency experiences, which were mostly socially orientated, caused the least anxiety.

Yamamoto et al. (1987) administered a questionnaire on perceived stressfulness of events to 1814 school-aged children from six countries. The questionnaire described 20 life events and the participants were asked to rate how stressful they thought this experience would be on a scale of one to seven. There was considerable similarity across nationalities in terms of the types of life events identified as stressful and the actual experiences of the young people in the study. Without exception, the experience of parental bereavement was rated as the most stressful experience. The birth of a sibling was universally rated as least upsetting. Other common potential stressors were:

- going blind
- being kept in the same class next year

- hearing my parents quarrel and fight
- wetting my pants in class
- being caught stealing something
- telling the truth but no one believing me.

A more recent and more extensive multinational study of adolescent 'worries' and their coping strategies is reported in Gibson-Cline (1996). Thirteen nations took part in the study which had a total sample size of 5067 13- to 15-year-olds, carefully chosen to represent different socio-economic groupings within the countries taking part. Children from the poorest and most disadvantaged communities were included as well as children from the most affluent and advantaged. The data were collected via an open-ended questionnaire which asked the young people to identify three events which they had found worrying or had made them feel pressured. They were then asked to describe: what they did about this problem; who they liked to help them; what qualities this person would have; and how they would help. The data were coded and analysed to produce 102 categories of problem; 37 classes of coping strategies; 42 types of desired helper; 390 types of desired helper qualities; and 27 modes of helping.

With the exception of minority females, from 16 to 35 per cent of males and females across all socio-economic backgrounds and different cultural groups reported schooling as causing most concern. Most of these concerns related to academic failure; concerns with schooling decreased in conjunction with poorer socio-economic status whereas family concerns increased. The other two most highly reported worries or pressures included problems with identity and family. Identity concerns were those which related to self-confidence and growing up – being afraid of being laughed at or being worried about being successful enough to support a family when older. The single most commonly reported type of family problem was parental strictness. The youngsters who lived in extreme poverty also listed money among their most common concerns. Increased effort, solution planning and seeking assistance were the most commonly reported coping strategies. Young people from higher socio-economic backgrounds were more likely to increase effort than youngsters from the poorest group. Only a minority of young people engaged in antisocial coping responses. Those who sought assistance, which was most frequent among the young people from the lowest socio-economic backgrounds, would locate helpers who could provide both information and social support. The most popular helpers were personal friends with parents coming second.

Research into stressors of infants and pre-school children have been more limited because of methodological restrictions. Hospitalization in an intensive care unit, neglect and pain are all acknowledged stressors of the newly born infant. For pre-school children poor day care, divorce, hospitalization, abuse or neglect, witnessing violence and loss of a parent have been linked with high stress (Barton and Zeanah, 1990). Barton and Zeanah also describe ways in which pre-schoolers can be helped to cope with stress more effectively. Providing information about the stressor so the child is prepared; encouraging expression of emotion directly or through play; maintenance of familiar routines and contact with attachment figures; and teaching problem-solving skills (which can be achieved from the age of 4 to 5 years onwards) are all helpful strategies for increasing effective coping in very young children.

It is not only traumatic events such as illness, abuse or bereavement which cause stress in children and young people. Problems which arise through everyday situations such as school, family and peer relationships can lead to high levels of anxiety and unhappiness.

Distinction between chronic, acute and neutral or general stressors

Trad and Greenblatt (1990) distinguish between chronic, acute and neutral stressors. They describe chronic stressors as creating 'an aura or background of stress against which an individual lives, or strives to live, a normal life' (p. 27). Chronic stressors would include long-term illness or disability, socio-economic deprivation, long-term parental arguing (perhaps prior to or following divorce), and repeated abuse. The consequences of chronic stress can be positive or negative. Children and young people who experience chronic stressors may experience low self-esteem, depression, anxiety disorders, accident proneness and a decline in general health. Alternatively, they may develop a whole array of coping strategies which actually result in them being more competent at handling adversity and stress in their lives. For example, Emery and Forehand (1994) note that the outcome of parental separation and divorce for most children is increased resilience (see Chapter 3).

Acute stressors are sudden, brief and intense. They include traumatic incidents, accidents, sudden injury, and the immediate impact of divorce or bereavement. These acute stressors often lead to a major change in the child's life for a short period of time. The negative effects of these may include nightmares, 'flashbacks', detachment, sleep disturbances, hypervigilance, anxiety and irritability. Some children who experience acute stressors develop post-traumatic stress disorder (PTSD). (This issue is also explored in Chapter 3). How children perceive their own role in these acute situations will shape the severity of the experience for them; if they perceive themselves as 'triumphing over adversity', their self-esteem can increase and the outcomes may be positive. Both chronic and acute stressors are described as non-normative in that they are not necessarily part of the usual range of experiences in childhood and adolescence.

The final group of stressors identified by Trad and Greenblatt are termed 'neutral'. Other researchers have described them as 'generic' or 'normative' (Compas et al., 1993). These are common experiences – 'daily hassles and small events' – which lead to a change in environment or routine: moving house, the birth of a sibling or a change of teacher. While most people would perceive acute and chronic stressors as adverse, neutral stressors are given a positive or negative connotation by the people directly involved. The accumulative effects of these more usual, quite frequent stressors have been linked to the development of psychological symptoms but not to maladjustment or psychopathology (DuBois et al., 1992).

These three broad categories of stressor are not mutually exclusive; they can occur together and one type of stressor can lead into another. Compas et al. (1993) suggest that chronic daily stress is a mediator between major life events and psychological distress. Both Pearlin (1991) and Rutter (1994) criticize much of the research into stress in adolescence and adulthood for focusing too much on individual stressful events and not considering sufficiently the probability that individuals will usually experience multiple stressors and that these could be interrelated.

Holmes and Rahe (1967) proposed that the general rate of change in a person's life could cause stress leading to illness. On the basis of this they developed their 'life changes' questionnaire which provides a summative score reflecting the overall quantity of change and major events. They predict that people who score highly are more likely to suffer the negative effects of stress. Cohen et al. (1987) tested the longitudinal effects of accumulative life events on 312 12- and 13-year-olds from five schools. They also collected data about life events experienced by the students' parents. They found that accumulative negative life events lead to an increase in anxiety and depression and a lowering of self-esteem. However, they also found that positive life events reduced the impact of the negative life events.

In summary, stressors can be chronic, acute or neutral. The outcome of experiencing chronic or acute stressors is not necessarily negative. 'Triumphing over adversity' can lead to increased self-esteem and competency as well as the development of effective coping strategies. Nevertheless, the combined impact of experiencing chronic daily stress and a sudden acute stressor may have greater negative impact than if either were experienced separately.

Immediate and long-term physical responses to stress

Some of the emotional and psychological consequences of stress have already been mentioned. The immediate physiological response to stress is universal. When under stress our bodies prepare for 'flight or fight' through changes in our physical state designed to improve our performance: blood supplies from the stomach, intestines and skin are sent to the brain and heart to improve judgement, decision making and breathing rate; extra energy is produced by increased release of glucose and fats into the bloodstream; and the sympathetic nervous system activates hormone release mechanisms which produce catecholamines leading to 'multi-physiological change' (Mason, 1975). Alternatively, a conservation-withdrawal response is activated by corticoids, leading to helplessness and depression sometimes called 'frozen watchfulness' (Henry, 1980). It is the repeated suppression of emotion and the maintenance of tension while the chemical reaction continues in our bodies which has been linked to stress-related diseases such as heart attacks, skin disorders, stomach and intestinal disorders (Eaton et al., 1981). While occasional stress responses enhance our performance for a short period of time, repeated exposure to stress can lead to permanent structural damage.

As well as actual physiological responses to stress, various psychosomatic symptoms may also develop. Ryan-Wenger (1990) reports a longitudinal examination of services used by 47,145 children in a private health care scheme: 17.3 per cent of diagnoses for children under the age of 11 were classed as psychosomatic. The most frequent forms of psychosomatic symptoms in school-aged children are stomach-ache and headache. Ryan-Wenger points out that most psychosomatic medicine is speculative and there is no real theory or knowledge about why or how these symptoms arise. The most common belief is that the electro-chemical neural circuits in the brain which interpret life experiences also influence physiological reactions.

Psychosomatic symptoms have been linked with non-supportive family or social environments, stressful life events and ineffective coping strategies. There is some evidence to suggest that the long-term physiological and psychosomatic effects of persistent daily hassles are more significant than major life events and traumas. The development of a psychosomatic symptom can result in more stress and, therefore, create a vicious cycle (see Figure 2.2 taken from Ryan-Wenger, 1990). Sears and Milburn (1990) suggest the following list of signs or symptoms of too much stress in school-aged children:

- regression to infantile behaviour – bed wetting, nail biting, thumb sucking
- uncharacteristic withdrawal – not talking to anyone, appearing depressed
- loss of motivation or inability to concentrate at school
- noticeable behaviour changes
- poor appetite and sleeplessness
- unexplained irritability
- physical ailments – headache, stomach-ache
- trouble getting along with peers.

Barton and Zeanah (1990) found typical pre-school responses to stressors included regression, increased attention seeking behaviour, social withdrawal and changes in play behaviour.

Children and young people who have experienced an extremely disturbing and life-threatening event such as a disaster, accident or violent crime may develop post-traumatic stress disorder (PTSD). This is explored further, with particular reference to sudden bereavement, in Chapter 3. PTSD usually follows from incidents which invoke intense fear, terror and helplessness (Tur-

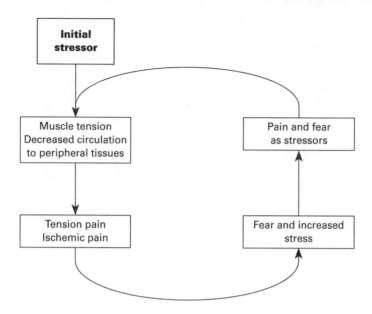

Figure 2.2 *Vicious cycle of psychosomatic symptom development and perpetuation (taken from Ryan-Wenger, 1990, p. 121)*

kel and Eth, 1990). The symptoms of PTSD in adults include re-experiencing the trauma, emotional numbing and increased arousal. In children and young people the symptoms vary with developmental phase (see Table 2.1). Pre-school children may seem withdrawn and subdued – they may even stop making any sounds. They are likely to regress, showing increased dependence on caregivers. They often re-enact the central events of the traumatic incident through play. As children get older they demonstrate a wider array of responses. Primary school aged children may experience concentration difficulties, deterioration of performance in school, confusion over the sequence of events, preoccupation with the small details of the incident, psychosomatic symptoms, sleep disturbance, bed wetting, immature behaviour, repetitive questioning about the incident. They may become rude, irritable, and provocative or withdrawn and clingy. Often their relationships with peers suffer, not only as a result of their inconsistent behaviour but also because they may try to engage friends in play re-enactments of the incident or imagined traumatic incidents, which seem strange and unwelcome to non-

Table 2.1   *Effects of PTSD on children and young people*

Pre-school children	Primary aged children	Adolescents
• withdrawn • subdued • mute • regression • increased dependence on care-takers • re-enacting traumatic incident through play	• concentration difficulties • deterioration of performance in school • confusion over the sequence of events • preoccupation with the small details of the incident • psychosomatic symptoms • sleep disturbance • bed wetting • immature behaviour • repetitive questioning about the incident • rude, irritable, provocative • withdrawn and clingy • re-enactment of the incident or imagined traumatic incidents	• hyper-vigilant • recurring thoughts and dreams about the incident • depression • helplessness • anxiety • survival guilt • rebellious and antisocial • drug or alcohol abuse • sexual behaviour • truancy • suicidal thoughts and behaviour

traumatized peers. Adolescent symptoms of PTSD are more similar to the responses of adults: they may become hyper-vigilant, have recurring thoughts and dreams about the incident, feel depressed, helpless, anxious or guilty because they survived and others did not. They may also become rebellious and anti-social, possibly engaging in drug or alcohol abuse, sexual behaviour, truancy or suicidal behaviour. Many children and young people who experience a traumatic incident are irrevocably changed. They become suddenly and brutally aware of mortality and the limitations of the protection their care-takers can offer. Nothing can change or soften that knowledge.

Stress leads to physiological, psychological, behavioural and emotional reactions. Children and young people may experience psychosomatic as well as psycho-social 'effects' of stress. Stress effects can vary in intensity from mild anxiety and temporarily increased arousal to the development of post-traumatic stress disorder.

Individual differences in responses to stress: resilience and vulnerability

Stress researchers have long been interested in the fact that some people face the most adverse conditions and thrive and gain from the experience, whereas other people in the same situation can be devastated and suffer short- and long-term negative effects. This interest has led to the generation of a large body of research into resilience and vulnerability. Risk factors increase the likelihood of a negative outcome for the individual. Protective factors are attributes of the person, the environment, and/or the situation which appear to prevent the development of negative outcomes, that is they increase resistance to risk or 'buffer' individuals against negative stress effects. Resilience is an individual characteristic reflecting the development of highly effective strategies for managing stress. Resilient people have often already demonstrated successful adaptation to stressful events and situations.

Protective factors are usually grouped into two categories:

- personal factors (for example, physical health, temperament, self-esteem, beliefs about control and competence)
- environmental resources (for example, family income, attachment to significant others, religious affiliation).

Werner (1989) noted that whereas risk factors are often embedded in culture, protective factors are more universal and less influenced by cultural difference. For children and young people, Garmezy and Rutter (1983) postulates the three most significant protective factors are:

- a positive disposition or personality
- a supportive family context
- an external support system which encourages and reinforces successful coping.

In 1980, Block and Block described 'ego resilient' children. These were children who were resourceful and creative in the development of solutions; were able to maintain constructive behaviour under stress; were able to process competing stimuli; and were adaptable to new situations. Breakwell et al. (1988) studied 210 16- to 18-year-olds and found that those individuals with low self-esteem and an external locus of control also reported higher levels of anxiety generally. Kimchi and Schaffner (1990) propose that while constitutional protective factors are more important in childhood, in adolescence it is interpersonal factors such as locus

Table 2.2   *Developmental profile of resilient youngsters (Kimchi and Schaffner, 1990)*

Developmental phase	Profile of resilient youngsters at this phase
Infancy	alert, responsive to people and objects, cheerful, readily gain caretaker's attention, easily soothed, good coper, intense drive and vigour, close bond with one primary individual for the first year
Pre-school	self-confident, independent, highly involved in play, good communicators, mobile, self-help skills, play vigorously, seek new experiences, can tolerate frustration and handle anxiety, take realistic risks but seek appropriate help, adaptive, relate well to peers and teachers
School age	good student, enjoy classmates and teachers, pursue hobbies, constructive, creative, enjoy humour, develop good friendships
Adolescence	well functioning, active, energetic, future orientated, responsible, caring, positive self-concept, internal locus of control, believe in self-help, high internalized values, socially perceptive and mature

of control, sense of control over the future, and planning to obtain realistic goals which are crucial. Table 2.2 shows the developmental profile of resilient youngsters as proposed by Kimchi and Schaffner, which they developed through a review of 24 studies into resilience among children and adolescents.

Werner (1989) monitored the impact of stressful life events on 698 Asian and Polynesian children from birth to the age of 30. They identified 72 children as resilient and carefully charted their development. In the primary years the resilient youngsters demonstrated good problem-solving and communication skills, were sociable, flexible and independent. As adolescents they had an internal locus of control, high self-concept and internalized values. They were achievement orientated, socially mature and perceptive, and nurturing in their approach to others. The autonomy and social orientation of these youngsters was notable from their pre-school year. Werner observed that they were adept at recruiting substitute parent figures.

An outgoing, extrovert manner is a recurring feature in research into resilience (see Kimchi and Schaffner, 1990, for a review). It seems that these resilient youngsters work on establishing good relationships with others, thereby creating a social network and developing a sense of social competence. They also have usually developed a secure attachment with one adult caregiver in infancy or have developed a relationship with one adult who has significant influence, such as a teacher. In other words, they have well-developed 'emotional intelligence' (Goleman, 1996). Research into successful living has suggested that traditional understandings of intelligence have been overly narrow, focusing on a small subset of verbal and mathematical skills (Gardner, 1993). Multiple intelligences have been identified, including interpersonal or emotional intelligence. Emotional intelligence includes five main domains:

- self awareness – knowing what you are feeling as you are feeling it
- managing emotions – handling emotions so they are appropriate, including under stressful circumstances
- self motivation – controlling emotions and impulses in order to achieve a goal
- empathy – recognizing and interpreting other people's emotions
- social competence – developing and managing relationships with others.

Children and young people who have developed these domains are more likely to manage stress constructively. Individuals differ in how well or badly they respond to stress. 'Buffers' or protective factors which reduce the negative effects of stress include: a positive disposition or personality, a supportive family context, and an external support system which encourages and reinforces successful coping.

Coping styles and strategies

Coping is another key element in the process of stress management. Coping can be defined as active efforts to resolve stress and to create reasonable solutions. How successfully or unsuccessfully we cope with stress will affect the extent and nature of the stress we experience. Hendren (1990) suggests that unsuccessful coping can, in the worst cases, lead to depression, suicide, substance abuse, eating disorders, and other mental and physical illnesses.

Pearlin (1991) describes coping as having three functions:

- to change or adapt the circumstances giving rise to stress
- to change the way we think and perceive the situation in ways which will minimize the potential for stress
- to control and relieve the symptoms of distress which arise from the stressors.

Coping may address one particular function, not necessarily all three. Pearlin points out that some life difficulties can be very resistant to individual coping efforts, particularly when stressors are embedded in an organization. For example, a student in a 'failing' school where many staff are demoralized or 'burnt out' will find it extremely difficult to change or adapt the situation causing stress. In these circumstances management of meaning and personal distress are more appropriate modes of coping than problem solving. Successful coping is highly specific to the situation and is also influenced by the actions of others involved in it. Pearlin summarizes:

> Multiple individuals within a role set may be experiencing, directly or indirectly, the same stressor circumstances; these stressors may unify the actors, or they may be the cause of conflict among them; they attempt to deal with the stressors similarly or differently; one's coping efforts may be supported, deflected, or opposed by others; and each may experience similar or different outcomes. (1991, p. 271)

Many researchers have divided coping strategies into two classifications – problem focused and emotion focused. Similar to Pearlin's functions, problem-focused strategies aim to change the stressor; emotion-focused strategies deal with the individual's emotional reactions to the stressor. Compas et al. (1988) looked at the problem-focused and emotion-focused strategies used by 130 10- to 14-year-olds. They found that adolescents used problem-focused and emotion-focused strategies in response to both academic and interpersonal relationship difficulties. As the students became older they generated and used more emotion-focused strategies. The use of problem focused strategies was more consistent with age. They found no significant gender differences overall but did note a tendency for girls to use more emotion-focused approaches when dealing with academic stressors. The experience of social stressors, but not academic stressors, correlated strongly with emotional and behavioural difficulties. In a later article Compas and his colleagues (Compas et al., 1991) explored the role of control-related beliefs in relation to how children perceive stressful events, how they attempt to cope with them, and how these affect them. Three types of judgements about personal control are seen as relevant. These are judgement about:

- means–ends relations
- personal competence
- control (either in terms of one's own ability to produce the desired outcome or the accuracy of one's appraisal of the controllability of the task).

In their studies of stress arising from peer relationship difficulties, they found that students with greater personal control were more likely to use problem-focused coping strategies; when their coping was successful, this in turn increased their sense of personal control. Emotional distress in these circumstances was reduced. This relationship is presented clearly by Skinner's schematic model of the competence system (Skinner, 1995; see Figure 2.3). Skinner proposes that control beliefs are developed through appraisal of strategy and personal capacity or competence following particular actions. In her research into perceived control in relation to friendships and academic success, Skinner found that when attributing academic success children were clear about the role of effort and academic ability. This was in marked contrast to their explanation of social success. The children described a wide range of actions which led to successful friendships but rarely mentioned effort or social skill. As Skinner writes: 'Children just

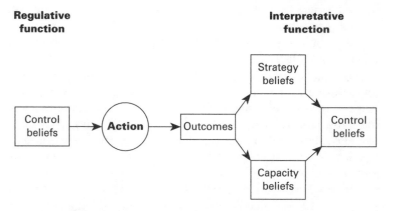

Figure 2.3   *A schematic of the competence system, including control, strategy and capacity beliefs (taken from Skinner, 1995, p. 96)*

weren't sure how these "friendship things" happened, although they were willing to speculate' (p. 162). This suggests metacognition about academic success is more developed than that about social success. This could reflect the lack of emphasis placed by schools on successful management of relationships.

Skinner suggests that coping is achieved through the regulation of behaviour, emotion and/or orientation. How this is achieved will vary according to whether the distress arises from oneself or the context and whether the situation is viewed as a threat or a challenge. When the stressor is perceived as a challenge, coping tends to be adaptive and constructive; when it is seen as a threat, it tends to be unconstructive, undermining or avoidant.

Rossman (1992) interviewed 345 6- to 12-year-olds. The children were asked what they did in stressful situations to make themselves feel better. Rossman found that their responses fell into two clear groups: utilizing peer or parental support and employing self-calming strategies. Younger children were more likely to distract themselves or avoid the situation as well as calm themselves and seek parental support. Girls were more likely to seek support from peers or parents and to express their distress.

Curry et al. (1992) compared 14- to 16-year-olds who had been identified through clinical referral as having suicidal thoughts with a control group of other young people. They found that the suicidal youngsters were less likely to employ problem-solving coping strategies.

Overholser (1992) focused specifically on the use of humour as a coping strategy among 19-year-old college students. He found that humour modified the relationship between life stress and adjustment when used occasionally. When humour was used consistently as a coping strategy it led to greater depression, loneliness and lower self-esteem. Overholser suggests this is because overuse of humour represents denial, is seen as socially inappropriate by others and is, therefore, alienating. Plancherel and Bolignini (1995) found that humour was most often used by boys as a coping strategy, with girls preferring social relationships and self-reliance.

Seiffge-Krenke (1993) surveyed 1028 12- to 19-year-olds from various cultures. Three main coping strategies emerged:

- active coping by means of social resources – for example, I discuss the problem with friends

- internal coping – for example, I analyse the problem myself and think of a variety of possible sources
- withdrawal – for example, I retreat because I am unable to change the situation.

Active coping, which involves efforts to manage the problem, emerged as the dominant style. Only one-fifth of all responses referred to withdrawal. Girls were more likely to talk about the problem, use peer support to resolve the problem, worry a lot, think about possible solutions and expect negative outcomes. Boys used less social support but anticipated more optimistic outcomes of stressful situations. They were less likely to withdraw from the situation or resign to it. However, when they faced very serious problems they were more likely to avoid the situation and engage in substance abuse. Reflective and active coping styles become more frequent with age. Despite these general trends, Seiffge-Krenke emphasized that each problem evoked its own specific pattern of coping strategies. She also noted considerable cultural variation. Similar results were noted by Olah (1995). In a study of 349 young men and 372 women aged 17 and 18 years old, Olah related low anxiety to constructive coping and high anxiety to avoidance. She also found that culture was the main influence on coping style. Seiffge-Krenke went on to compare the coping styles of the subjects in the survey with results obtained from a smaller group of disturbed adolescents who had been referred to a clinical psychology service. Use of withdrawal as a coping strategy was significantly higher.

Gore and Eckenrode (1994) criticize research into coping for failing to investigate the reciprocity of relationships between different coping strategies or their interchangeability. For example, they ask can deficits in social esteem be made up for with high levels of academic self-esteem? Children can be successful in school in different ways, for example, through academic, athletic or social success. Is it sufficient that the child is successful in just one arena to maintain self-esteem and sense of competency and, therefore, protect against negative effects of stress? Gore and Eckenrode go on to suggest that perhaps it is not exactly how one copes that makes the difference between positive and negative outcomes, but the fact that the person does something at all.

Clearly, coping is a crucial factor in determining the outcomes of stressful experiences for the individual. Fortunately, both resilience and effective coping can be developed in children and young people, and subsequent chapters will explore ways in which adults can work with youngsters to increase protective factors as well as supporting them through crisis or trauma. Coping is a complex process during which a young person will draw upon internal resources (ability to generate solutions, self-esteem, sense of control and competency) and external resources (social support networks, environmental influences). The most appropriate ways of coping are subject to individual difference and the nature of the stressful situation.

3

CHILDREN AND GRIEF

Not to educate ourselves and our children about our relationship with death means not educating ourselves and them about
life. It is dangerous to do so, and not because of death – sooner
or later we will all die – but because it profoundly affects the
quality of our life, both before and after we have become
bereaved. The best preparation for bereavement is death-
education. The best preparation for life is to relate death to our
ways and values of living.

(Gersie, 1991, pp. 38–9)

The wood burns away, but the fire goes on forever.

(Ancient Somali proverb)

Unless a wheat grain falls into the earth and dies it remains
only a single grain; but if it dies it yields a rich harvest.

(Gospel of St John, 12: 24)

Responses to loss

We saw in Chapter 1 the crucial part which close relationships
have on the emotional well-being of the child. Children need to
form affectional bonds with others to ensure their emotional
security and physical safety. We discussed the nature of attachments and the impact on the child of the loss of an attachment
figure. In this chapter we look at grief and the particular ways in
which children are affected when they have to cope with the death
of someone whom they know. First, we explore how adults can
help children to deal with the loss of a family member or peer in
a sensitive, caring way. Next we look at bereavement and the
processes of grieving, both within the family and in other settings
such as schools. We also consider the impact on children of

witnessing or being close to a death, particularly a sudden or violent death. Finally, we discuss the concept of resilience in the face of loss.

James Robertson carried out a classic series of studies in collaboration with John Bowlby (Robertson, 1952) at a time when the importance of parent–child contact was not fully realized. Robertson and Robertson (1972) demonstrated the extreme emotional distress of a two-year-old separated from her mother through hospitalization. Their observations in a series of films on such separations from parents indicated a typical sequence of emotional responses on the part of the child. First there was protest, when the child would cry and call out for the absent parent, and when attempts by hospital staff to comfort him or her would usually fail. Second, there was withdrawal, when the children became apathetic and withdrawn. Third, there was detachment, when there was an apparent recovery in the sense that the child appeared superficially to relate to hospital staff and other children. When reunited with their parents, these children often reacted in an atypical way – with cold rejection, angry tantrums or unusual clinginess. This behaviour could last for a long time.

Later research by the Robertsons showed that these reactions to separation could be alleviated if one of the parents or another trusted adult visited frequently, or even stayed in the hospital, or where as far as possible the children were prepared emotionally for the separation. In other words, where the child's distress was acknowledged and treated as a normal and understandable grieving reponse, it was easier to help such children deal with their feelings. By contrast, where children were discouraged from expressing grief – told to 'pull themselves together', 'cheer up' or 'be a brave boy or girl' – there was a much greater likelihood of longer-term distress.

The Robertsons's studies were controversial because the researchers did not intervene to help the distressed children at the time, but the research gave incontrovertible evidence about the strength of the emotions which children felt when they were separated from their parents. Similar responses have been reported in many other studies, including research on children's emotional responses to fostering and adoption, and on children affected by parental separation or divorce. There are also implications for our understanding of action which adults can take to alleviate the distress of children who are in the process of grieving over the death of someone close to them.

Bereavement

If a child experiences prolonged separation from a loved one or loss through death of such a person, it is necessary for him or her to go through a period of mourning, just as an adult would. Children, like adults, are likely to react with behavioural changes when they are coming to terms with the death of someone close to them. For example, in a study of the impact on families of sudden infant death syndrome (Dent et al., 1996), 75 per cent of parents reported that they had noticed behavioural changes in the siblings of the dead baby. These symptoms included withdrawal, stealing, sleeping problems, regressive behaviour, attention-seeking and putting on weight. When a child dies, the feelings of the surviving siblings may well be ambivalent. The parents may be too distressed to offer enough support to the other children in the family; in some families it is very difficult to talk about the death (Newman et al., 1997). Many families in this situation say that they would welcome support in dealing with the distress of the surviving siblings.

In order to understand children's grief, we need to be aware of their reactions at different ages; their cognitive concept of separation and loss; and their grief reactions, including physical and psychological symptoms. There are well-established ways in which adults can offer help and support, but it is important to remember that these interventions must be provided with care and empathy for the child's distress.

Children, like adults, experience deep feelings of grief over the loss of a loved one but, because they do not always – on the surface – appear to be upset, some children can give the impression that they do not care. Nothing could be further from the truth. Because they are vulnerable to emotions of fear relating to a sense of abandonment, especially if the dead person is a close member of the family, there are likely to be times when they are so overwhelmed by the event that they need to take time out from grieving. Euphemisms like 'Grandpa's asleep' or 'Mummy's gone away' add to the child's confusion and he or she may become unnecessarily afraid or anxious about normal activities in everyday life like going to bed at night or seeing a parent going out for a short time.

How younger children understand the concept of death

Children from the age of 3 to 7 years demonstrate 'magical thinking' around the concept of death by, for example, believing that their own actions can in some way cause the dead person to come alive again. This egocentric perspective is a normal part of development but can have damaging emotional outcomes for the child in the context of bereavement if the irrational thoughts are not addressed. (Adults too can, of course, retain magical thoughts about the causes of death, such as: 'Why did God punish me in this way?' or 'What did I do to deserve this loss?'.) Children may come to believe that their actions or thoughts caused the death, so it is important for adults to attend to the child's magical thinking in order to help deal with irrational feelings of guilt. For example, young children may believe that, because they had at times harboured angry thoughts about the dead person, they may have actually caused the person to die; alternatively they may think that if they behave very well, the dead person will come back. They may also fear that their 'bad thoughts' may cause another death in the family and so repress natural feelings of anger and upset about their loss. One reason for the perpetuation of such unfounded beliefs may be that at the time of the death the adults were too preoccupied with their own grief to listen to the child's fears and anxieties. Children at this stage of development are especially vulnerable. Although they are beginning to understand death with their minds, they are unlikely to have sufficient emotional reserves to protect themselves from the full impact of their loss.

Children's questions about death (for example, 'It's cold under the ground. Is Daddy wearing warm socks?') can often be very concrete and indicate the difficulty which they have in understanding the nature of death. It is essential to explain clearly to the child that the dead person no longer has feelings, is not cold or in pain, and does not need food any more. Young children are often curious about what happens to the body and it is quite acceptable to give information on the different procedures for burial or for cremation. Dyregrov (1991) quotes examples of children asking when Mummy is coming back or repeating questions like, 'Where can we get the bus to heaven?', so expressing their yearning to be reunited with the dead parent. These are difficult questions to answer, especially when many adults themselves are ambivalent about the possibility of an afterlife. Hayworth (1989) suggests that children are unlikely to be comforted either by adult statements about the finality of death, vague explanations about the dead person being in heaven which are not founded in genuine belief, or by abstract statements about immortality. She recommends instead that adults give responses which take account of the poignancy of separation through death while still being honest about what they can and what they cannot accept about the idea of being reunited, on some level, with the dead person.

Case study

A 6-year-old attended the funeral of her great-grandfather. Her family explained that great-grandfather had died and this meant that he didn't breathe, speak or move any more and that his body would be put into the ground. She was reminded, 'it is like when your budgie died earlier this year'. She responded, 'But I hear my budgie singing in the garden every day. He watches over me.'

On arrival at the funeral parlour, older relatives went to 'pay their last respects'. The little girl became insistent that she too wanted 'to see the body'. Her family agreed and she went into the chapel of rest. She peered into the coffin at her great-grandfather and began to poke at his chest. 'But where is his body? I can only see his face.' she asked. In the church, as the coffin was brought to the altar, she said to her family, 'That's my great-grandad in there. His bosoms don't move anymore and you can only see his face.'

A few days later she said thoughtfully, 'Great-grandad's watching over me, just like my budgie.'

Images may be helpful in conveying the concept of the dead person no longer being in the body. Children at this stage are also quite capable of understanding symbolic acts like laying flowers on the grave or scattering the ashes. The meaning of symbolic rituals can be understood by children at some level and give a focus for the mourning process, for example through the use of holy water, incense or earth. In a similar way, poetic metaphors can help the child begin to understand the distinction between the person as they were when alive and as they are now that they are dead:

Remember how the tree's leaves die and then fall off the tree onto the ground? They are still beautiful but they are not alive and green after they have died. We will always remember and love Tommy even though we cannot see him or play with him anymore. (Hayworth, 1989, p. 30)

It may be appropriate to say that we do not know whether there is a possibility of being with the dead person again or, at a suitable point, to explore with the child the idea of separation between body and spirit:

> When a person dies, the body becomes an empty house. Most people believe that the spirit which was living with the body goes to heaven. Our spirit is not a part of the body. It is with our spirit that we able to give love and receive love. The spirit or soul never wears out. We cannot see someone's spirit, nor can we see heaven. We believe that we have a spirit and that there is a heaven. This is what we call faith. People of all religions believe that we have a spirit that lives on after our bodies have died. (Kirkwood, in Ward, 1989, p. 31)

Even though a child does not have direct experience of bereavement in the family, it is likely that they will still be aware of issues around the differences between life and death. Young children may begin to think about mortality through the death of a classmate, by hearing about the death of a friend's relative, or through the death of a prominent figure. Children around the world will have seen the public demonstrations of grief which followed the deaths in 1997 of Diana, Princess of Wales, and Mother Teresa; many will have been a part of the collective mourning experience, viewed the religious ceremonies on the television, and seen spontaneous demonstrations of sorrow in public places.

Case study

Seven-year-old Laura was sitting on a railway station platform, waiting for a train. She began to talk about holidays. She said suddenly, 'Kelly and I have decided we are never going to Paris.' Further exploration of her reasons for this revealed that this was because Princess Diana had died in Paris and the girls had begun to think about Paris as an unsafe place – a place where people die. In the following month, Laura became obviously more fearful of danger and alert to media coverage of murders and accidents. She would ask questions about strangers, about walking alone, and about children and parents being killed. It became clear that the huge amount of publicity surrounding Princess Diana's death had alerted Laura and her friends to the possibility of sudden, unexpected death and they had then become increasingly aware of other incidents which resulted in people, and in particular children, dying suddenly and violently. This morbid phase lasted for about two months after the Princess's death.

Older children and the concept of death
From the age of 7 through adolescence, children's mourning is very similar to that of adults. Worden (1991), writing about the

grieving process, argues that there are four tasks of mourning which children, like adults, need to accomplish before it can be said that the process of mourning has been completed (Worden, 1991, p. 125). The four tasks identified by Worden are:

To accept the reality of the loss;
To work through the pain of grief;
To adjust to an environment in which the dead person is missing;
To relocate emotionally the deceased person and move on in life.

Older school-age children are moving out of egocentric modes of thinking and are able more clearly to understand at a cognitive level the nature of death, but they may be less willing to express their feelings. Their mourning process may not end in the same way as an adult's since grief may be reactivated in adult life by related experiences of separation and loss, and unresolved or partially resolved issues may need to be worked through again.

As with younger children, there are wide individual differences in young people's responses to a death. In the first instance, on hearing the news of a death, they can respond with disbelief, with anger or protest, or with apparent apathy and a studied involvement in their usual activites. When children do not respond in the expected way, it is easy to make mistaken inferences about the depth of the child's feeling or to misunderstand the child's behaviour or demeanour. Boys are more likely to have difficulty in expressing their feelings than girls. Dyregrov (1991) reports her study of school children's responses to the sudden violent death of their teacher. The girls cried more, showed more overt signs of distress and were able to write more about the event. Most of the girls reported that they had confided their feelings to a friend; fewer than 40 per cent of the boys had done this.

As with younger children, the first task of grieving is to confront the fact that the dead person has gone and will not come back. In the early stages of bereavement it can be very difficult for the young person not to deny the loss has taken place. The denial takes a number of forms. The young person may enter into a numbed state which can go on for days or even weeks, may talk to the dead person, or may imagine that they can see the dead person. They may, alternatively, deny the importance of the loss by saying, 'I don't miss him much' or 'We weren't that close'. These are strategies which young people devise for protecting themselves from the pain of loss. They may even appear to take time out of grieving – they may cry and then act in a seemingly normal way as if nothing had happened. This can be mistakenly interpreted as a lack of feeling when it actually means that the young person is unable to cope with the pain of grief for as long a time as an adult can. The whole process can take time until the acceptance is integrated at both cognitive and emotional levels.

The role of the teacher

At a time when parents are also suffering acute stress it can be difficult to be supportive to children who are reacting with anger, fear, aggression, panic, regressed behaviour, or who are showing a sudden deterioration in school work or having difficulties in peer relationships. These reactions can easily be misinterpreted by adults close to the death who may be so preoccupied with their own grief that they are not in a position to offer support. This is where other adults, such as teachers, can play a special part in creating an atmosphere of calm and trust for the distressed child, providing familiar routines at a time of chaotic emotions. They can also prepare in advance for the probability that, from time to time, there will be a grieving young person in the class by helping all children to understand the concept of death and dying, by raising awareness of the feelings that accompany mourning, and by ensuring that the bereaved child's grief is not compounded by rejection on the part of insensitive peers.

Case study

Charles was in the process of sitting his GCSE examinations when his father's health deteriorated rapidly. His parents tried to shield him from the seriousness of the illness and both urged him to concentrate on his studies and try to do his best. Charles was a good student and succeeded in keeping up to his usual high standard of achievement. He felt especially pleased at the way in which he answered the General Science paper and hurried home to tell his parents. He arrived to find that his father had died that morning. His mother had delayed telling him since 'there seemed no point in upsetting him as he was about to sit an important exam'. She appeared calm and in control of her feelings. She told Charles that now he was the man of the house and that his father would be very proud of the responsible way in which he had conducted himself during this difficult time.

Charles's mother took care of all the funeral arrangements herself since, as she said, 'Charles is not a believer and never attends church.' On the day of the funeral, while the adults attended the church service, Charles went out for a walk and, to his own surprise, passed the church just as the mourners were coming out. He asked himself first, 'Who are these people?' and then answered his own

question out loud, 'Oh yes, they're at Dad's funeral.' In the following days his aunt commented in Charles's hearing that he seemed
not to be deeply affected by the loss and 'was coping well'. He felt
very angry but said nothing.

His examination results were excellent, and he was praised for his
strength in carrying on with his life despite his loss. But a few
months later he had unusually vehement outbursts of anger over
trivial episodes. He believed that he was being avoided by his peers
and became known as someone whom it was easy to offend. He
became increasingly withdrawn from social life and turned more
and more to his studies. Despite this, his academic performance
began to drop. Charles's science teacher became worried and called
him in for a chat. At long last he was able to begin to explore his
deep sense of loss. One of the most helpful things which he was able
to do through the intervention of his teacher was to design his own
special mourning ritual for his father.

There was a distinct danger that Charles had been pushed too
quickly into an adult supportive role and so denied the opportunity to be in touch with his own grieving processes. Charles's
teacher recognized this and acknowledged Charles's strength
while at the same time giving him strategies for keeping alive the
memory of the dead person through such mementoes as letters,
photographs and other reminders. Most importantly, he gave him
time and space to talk about his dead father.

Adjusting to an environment in which the dead person is missing

As Charles's case indicated, the bereaved young person may feel
obliged to take on new roles and develop new skills. In the
process, if too much is expected at once, the young person may
behave in atypical ways. Charles's school work deteriorated and
his relationships with classmates altered. Over time this behaviour
usually changes and the child goes back to normal patterns;
however, if the child's behaviour is not dealt with sympathetically,
he or she may find it difficult to move on. Adjustment to the
world as a place which is no longer always safe can be a very
threatening experience which challenges fundamental values and
beliefs. Working through this task means that the young person
must recognize the new circumstances, revise his or her model of
the world and accept that he or she has changed.

At this stage, children or adolescents will need support in both
keeping alive thoughts and memories of the dead person and

fulfilling the need to 'move on' emotionally. Adults and peers can help them 'find an appropriate place for the dead in their emotional lives – a place that will enable them to go on living effectively in the world' (Worden, 1991, p. 17). This is not always achieved easily, especially if the loss is of a close friend or relative. The 'relocation' involves having a place for thoughts and memories of the dead person which do not prevent the child from continuing with important current relationships. It does not mean denying the loss or abandoning the memories of the dead person, but engaging once more with the emotional bonds of the present. It means not fearing to love again because of the pain of loss; it means that life goes on and it is possible to think of the dead person without unbearable pain.

This mourning process takes time. It is insensitive to think that a child can move quickly through the grieving process. It is impossible to give precise times since each person will approach the tasks of mourning in their own way, but it is important to be aware of the child's emotional responses. Apparent recovery from loss may mask unresolved feelings of sadness and despair.

The mourning process can be said to be finished when the child rediscovers the joy of living, feels optimistic – when laughter returns. However, feelings of sadness will always remain and it is important to acknowledge these feelings when they appear. The sensitivity with which adults handle this process is a key factor. Here Rebecca Abrams, whose father died when she was 18, points out that bereavement is not something which a person soon 'gets over'; rather, it takes time:

> I wish someone had explained to me about time when my father died. I wish someone had thought to tell me that a month is not long enough to get used to the death of someone who has been central to your life for eighteen years. It would have helped so much to know that however normal I might appear after a month, a year would not be long enough to begin to feel normal again. (Abrams, 1992, p. 76)

What adults can do
It is essential for adults to be aware of the different developmental needs of the bereaved child as well as the particular and characteristic ways in which that child mourns. The single most important thing is to listen to the child: to give the child time and listen to their story in whatever form it comes. As the case studies show, props like photographs or mementoes can help the process;

the media of story, play and drawing may give the child ways of symbolizing incomprehensible or overwhelming feelings.

It is also important for the adult to be aware of the non-verbal ways of expressing grief and to be sensitive to them, even if at times they are disturbing. The child may, for example, be involved in regression to an earlier developmental stage. Some children become incontinent, or have nightmares, or become afraid to be left in the dark. When these symptoms appear, the adults can be most helpful by ensuring that the child feels secure and loved, whatever he or she does. It is important not to punish the child for regressive behaviour, tantrums or atypical outbursts of anger soon after a bereavement.

The adult needs to demonstrate care and concern through practical help, by listening, by allowing time for tears, by encouraging the child to move on when the time is right, by being tolerant and accepting when the child regresses, and, very importantly, by praising the child for strength and resilience when this emerges. Lendrum and Syme (1992) identify a whole range of ways in which adults and peers can help and support children through the grieving process. While they recognize that counselling may be necessary for some aspects of the process or in extreme cases, much of the support is best done by trusted adults and friends the child knows well and with whom he or she feels safe. Most bereaved children will be helped to resolve their grief through the following three types of intervention:

1 Children's questions about the death must be answered openly, in a factual way and at the time when they ask them. For example, breaking the news of a death to a child must be done with care, and the words should be direct and simple. Euphemisms (for example, 'You have lost your mother.') are much less helpful than factual information (for example, 'Your mother is dead.'), blunt as the facts may sound.

2 They need to be allowed to participate in the family's grieving. The preparations for the funeral must involve the children in some way, and there are many rituals surrounding a death which can be adapted to the age and individual needs of the child. Some families go to great lengths to protect children from the sorrow of death, but it is impossible to avoid the intense distress of losing a parent or someone close to the child. A silence around the event or a deliberate avoidance of mentioning the topic can only prolong the mourning process

which the child has to work through. Strong feelings of grief can be reactivated at anniversaries or at other important family occasions such as weddings or Christmas. It is often helpful to devise a ritual or commemoration at such times in order to help the child deal with emotions of grief and give expression to them.

3   They need the on-going security of a parent or other adult to provide comfort and support. The everyday routines of family life can be reassuring to the child.

Chapman (1997) recalls the grief experienced by her and her three children when her husband died suddenly from a brain haemorrhage at the age of 37 during a family holiday. Her account demonstrates one way in which a parent could share his or her own grief with the children and help them deal with theirs. With the help and support of a friend in the holiday group the whole family stayed with the body, despite the attempts of the authorities to remove it. They talked about the death together and cried together. Once home, she thought carefully about how best to involve the children in the funeral:

> When we returned to England, we had an open coffin at the funeral parlour, and each of our children gave him a gift. The older two gave him a Tintin book and Hamish gave him one of the sweets that he had with him. They could think of him having something precious to take away with him. They were then able to relate to him being in the coffin when it was lowered into the grave. Later, we set up a memorial fund for re-landscaping their school playground. Paul was a builder and had done some work on the school grounds before he died. Friends and family donated £5000, and it made the children realise that he was very valued. (Chapman, 1997, p. 8)

The role of peers

The company of other children can also be a source of great comfort. Many bereaved children emphasize the helpfulness of other children in alleviating the pain of loss. Cantacuzino (1997) reports on the work of charitable organizations which run holiday camps for bereaved children since it has been found that talking to other bereaved peers is one of the most therapeutic forms of intervention in coming to terms with a death. The peer group can also be extremely helpful for children who have witnessed traumatic deaths and are suffering post-traumatic stress as a result (Yule and Williams, 1990).

Quarmby (1993) had similar findings when he ran a group of six sessions for bereaved adolescents, all of whom had experienced the death of a parent. The group sessions gave the young people time to talk about their feelings around the bereavement, and all participants reported that the process of talking in a safe, trusted group gave them the freedom to disclose painful memories which had not previously been shared with anyone. One of Quarmby's findings was, however, that not all peers are helpful in these circumstances. Members of his group reported that bereavement had been experienced as leading to a loss of status among peers at school. As we argue in Chapter 5, the peer group is a resource to young people in distress but only some of the roles adopted by members of a peer group will be supportive. It is essential that adults and more sympathetic peers watch out for unhelpful responses from other children. The adults who are close to the bereaved children and young people should also have certain attitudes and skills, and a supportive understanding stance to the loss.

Coping with death at school

It is best if schools are prepared for the fact that at some point they will have to deal with deaths. Most schools now have a policy on the topic and are ready to deal with death or other traumatic events – a far more preferable situation than a reaction at a time of crisis when many of the people involved in caring for the children may well be in a state of shock themselves. Teachers are an important resource in caring for children when a death affects the whole school, with a unique contribution to make for the following reasons (adapted from Dyregrov, 1991, p. 81):

- teachers know the individual child and their personality
- teachers know the 'culture' within each class
- teachers are experts in providing children with knowledge, more so than psychologists and psychiatrists
- teachers know how to help children using a variety of expressive means to deal with critical events
- teachers are well-known and trusted by the children.

The following case study is an example of how one school responded when a 13-year-old boy died as a result of a tragic accident (the names and circumstances have been changed to ensure anonymity).

Case study

On the day immediately following the death, the Headteacher wrote a letter to the parent(s) of every pupil in the school which contained information about the death, the circumstances of the accident, details about the speed with which the emergency services came to the scene, and the time at which the pupil died. He wrote:

> As you can imagine, the whole school community is shocked and saddened by this tragedy. We have been supported today by trained counsellors who have been helping staff in talking with the students both in groups and individually.

He went on to outline ways in which the school was acting to offer opportunities for staff and students to seek help and information:

> We have decided to close the school tomorrow as a mark of respect for John and to enable the investigation into the accident to be completed as quickly as possible. The school will be open tomorrow for any student who wishes to come in to meet with staff or counsellors to talk about any feelings which they would like help with . . . We have arranged for a telephone help line to be available tomorrow and all next week during half term. Any parent or student who wishes to speak to someone or ask any questions will be able to ring this number.

He outlined proposals for a range of ways to express sorrow both individually and as a community: 'I will write to you again about the arrangements for a memorial service for John'. A leaflet enclosed with the letter, entitled 'Coping with Traumatic Death', gave information about common feelings which bereaved children and their families might experience, mentioning specifically that it can be helpful to cry; giving factual information on physical and mental sensations which might occur immediately after the accident, and in the days and weeks following it; and offering guidelines on the need to talk about feelings rather than bottle them up. The leaflet also outlined some practical suggestions for action which might be helpful for those who were closest to John, those who saw the accident, members of his immediate peer group, his teachers and for those who were indirectly affected by his death, for example through the evocation of their own losses. The leaflet ended:

> The sudden death of a pupil in the school has had a profound impact on the entire school community. It has been the greatest shock for those directly involved and for those who witnessed it. It has had a great impact too on parents and teachers. Support is available for them. Such an event will have stirred up feelings for the whole school, including staff and students who were not present at the accident; they too will need to be heard.

The death was commemorated in a special assembly which gave the opportunity for the family of the dead boy and his teachers and peers to gather together to express their grief and consider what the loss meant to each one, with opportunities for special tributes to be paid both by those who were closest to him and by other members of the community. The family were involved at all stages and said how moving it was to be able to share their grief with staff and students in the school. Later, a memorial was set up in the playground where John had loved playing football.

These symbolic acts and the experience of collective grieving facilitated the process of mourning, gave some emotional release, and provided a way of giving direct expression to inner thoughts and feelings.

The impact of a critical incident on a community

All local authorities have Emergency Planning Arrangements which come into effect following a major incident. However, on a day-to-day basis there are many critical incidents which do not count as 'major' incidents but nevertheless have a significant impact, not only on those immediately involved and who are directly affected, but also on other people throughout the community.

Recently, we have become more aware of this wider impact and this has led services to support communities in their endeavours to develop strategies and approaches for helping to manage the impact of a critical incident. Educational psychology services have begun to be more centrally involved in supporting schools following a critical incident. Houghton (1996) carried out a survey of all educational psychology services in the UK. She found that 65 per cent of all of the educational psychology services who responded (n = 91; 76 per cent of all services) had been involved in supporting schools during critical incidents during the previous three years. Over half of the reported cases had arisen through the violent death of a child. These were mostly due to road traffic accidents, but 10 per cent were murders. In 28 per cent of these cases, the death (including four of the murders) had been witnessed by other children.

It was predominantly the Headteacher who requested involvement from the educational psychology service. The main role of the educational psychology service was to advise, support and 'enable' school staff to cope and manage the incident as well as offering counselling to children, staff and sometimes parents. Cameron et al. (1995) describe in more detail the kinds of support offered in four separate critical incidents. In one of these incidents the educational psychologists facilitate a staff meeting where staff talk about how they felt, how they had heard the news of the incident, how they reacted, and their fears and concerns. An important feature of this meeting was the 'normalizing' of the bereavement process. The staff meeting was followed by an 'open line' – an assured telephone contact which was continually available. This was not used and the school staff went on to deal effectively with the short and long-term impact of the incident. The value of early support to staff, which helps them to manage the incident and therefore regain/maintain control, is apparent and is a common feature of this kind of intervention.

Cameron et al. summarize the primary roles of the educational psychologists as:

- Helping the Headteacher or school management team to identify those people to whom priority should be given and to draw up a rough plan of action.
- Discussing how to mobilize and develop within school support systems.
- Helping children and adults to utilize therapeutic concepts and techniques from psychology which will help them to recognize the normal range of reactions to an incident, mobilize inner resources and prevent the onset of post-traumatic stress disorder.
- Briefing staff so they can capitalize on therapeutic opportunities which arise naturally during classroom activities.

They suggest that the following set of principles should underpin any kind of intervention:

- availability and accessibility – schools know who to contact and how
- immediate response to first contact
- needs assessment prior to action
- a sound understanding of post-traumatic stress syndrome and bereavement processes
- ability to be able to offer counselling in a planned way
- good liaison and coordination with other agencies
- a plan for media handling.

The above obviously require some forward planning and many psychology services now have a policy or set of guidelines for supporting schools in critical incidents. The following is an excerpt from Buckinghamshire Educational Psychology Service's guidelines (Norman et al., 1997):

What the Educational Psychology Service (EPS) will offer

In each area team, there are Educational Psychologists who are members of the 'Crisis Response Group' and who have had experience of supporting the school after a critical incident. It is proposed that the EPS offer the following services:

- Advice, support and training to schools to enable them to prepare for a critical incident.
- Advice and support (through direct involvement) immediately after a critical incident.
- Where appropriate, critical incident stress debriefing.
- Information for schools about statutory and voluntary bodies able to provide appropriate longer term counselling and support.
- Guidance to the LEA on action to be taken following a critical incident.
- Advice to the LEA on its policy for responding to critical incidents affecting schools.
- In-service training to develop schools knowledge of the process of grief and loss and the impact of critical incidents on a school community.

What the EPS will do

The impact of a critical incident may overwhelm the normal coping strategies of individuals and communities. Any response to a school affected by a traumatic event must take into account the effects on children both immediately after the event and in the longer term.

The Service accepts the need for a swift response to a request from a school after a critical incident. The first contact will probably be through the school's link educational psychologists. We recognise the need for a flexible and sensitive range of responses based on our psychological understanding of the reactions and needs of the children and adults involved.

In most cases the link educational psychologist will retain responsibility for work undertaken in the school. (The link EP has the right to opt out of this role. This would especially be the case if they themselves had experienced a recent bereavement or trauma.) The link EP will be actively supported by colleagues who have relevant training and/or relevant experience.

The involvement of the team will cover the following areas:

- An assessment of the situation to establish the facts and a planning meeting with the school management to agree on action and priorities.
- Advice to staff on how to support children after a traumatic event.

- Work with staff to help them to cope better with their experiences.
- Support for children employing techniques such as 'critical incident stress de-briefing'.
- Work with school staff and other adults (e.g. parents) using psychological techniques to help them to cope with their stress more effectively.
- Advice to parents about how they can support their children at home through listening to them etc..
- Longer term counselling with children or adults where it is felt to be appropriate.
- Liaison with other agencies (e.g. emergency planning officer, social services department, voluntary agencies such as CRUSE) as appropriate, to ensure the full range of support which a school might benefit from is made available.
- Debriefing sessions for the educational psychologists involved.
- Support from the full EPS team to allow the planned work of the EPs involved to be covered.
- An evaluation of the team's involvement to identify learning points and improve future responses.

Case study of a critical incident and its impact on the school community

A small village community were shocked to find that a teacher had committed suicide. He had lived in the village all his life and taught at the secondary school he had attended as a pupil. He had lived alongside many of the students he had taught and they had witnessed the arrival of the ambulance and police. The next day students and teachers arrived at school in a shocked and distressed state. The previous evening people from the village had begun to lay flowers at the school entrance and so on arrival at school everyone was reminded of the tragic death. Coincidentally, it was the first anniversary of a terrible school tragedy in which many young children had been killed in Dunblane, Scotland. The morning papers, radio and TV had been full of reminders of this awful event and this heightened the emotional response of those bereaved people in this small, tightly knit community.

Earlier that morning the Headteacher met with the school's link educational psychologist and the local vicar to discuss how he should handle the day. The educational psychologist explained to him the range of responses he might expect from staff and students and discussed ways in which he could manage the day. All agreed it was very important that students and staff should feel he was in control of the situation, that usual routines should be maintained as much as possible but that, within these parameters, there should be space for people to grieve for the sad loss.

The Headteacher led a staff briefing during which he outlined the known facts of their colleague's death. The school's link educational psychologist and the local vicar were introduced as being available to support staff in their support for students. The psychologist described the usual reaction to a sudden bereavement and discussed with staff some of the things they or their students may be feeling or experiencing, both on that day and in the future. The staff went to register their classes and then to lead them to a special assembly. The deputy headteacher registered the dead colleague's form, accompanied by the vicar and the psychologist. They spent some time with each class, so that everyone, including the teacher, was able to express their reactions to their form tutor's death.

The assembly was a dignified and solemn event. As the children and staff spent a few moments in quiet remembrance of their colleague and teacher, one child began to cry openly and loudly. Quiet sobs and sniffs began to spread across the hall and accompanied the departure of the students to their classes. This flood of tears presented some practical problems – there was insufficient toilet tissue and a member of staff was quickly dispatched to the local supermarket to purchase more toilet tissue and some boxes of tissues which could be made available throughout the school.

Some students were reluctant to continue with their classes and walked in twos or threes around the school comforting each other. The Headteacher responded quickly, urging students to return to their usual classes and encouraging all to accept that they might cry during the day – this was fine and there were tissues in every class – but they should as far as possible stick to routine. This adherence to routine yet also allowing people to express their emotions helped everyone to manage their grief without repressing it. The sense of mutual support and community was very evident and enabled the school to move on.

Critical Incident Debriefing

One of the important 'healing' and coping processes for people who are involved in a critical incident is to talk about and review impressions and reactions arising during and after the incident. Critical Incident Debriefing is a structured procedure to facilitate this process. It is now often incorporated into plans for responding to critical incidents and should be available for all those involved, including people such as police officers and rescue workers.

Critical Incident Debriefing should be carried out by people who have been trained to use the technique; in this section we give a brief outline of what is involved. Critical Incident Debriefing does not replace talking to colleagues, friends and relatives about the incident. During the incident, talking with others about what is happening and one's emotional reactions build support and caring. This is called 'defusing' and has been identified as a helpful and important element of successful coping.

Case study

Sahid was involved in a nasty car accident on his way to school. He was injured and the driver of the other car was killed. Sahid's family encouraged him to talk about what had happened and how he felt. He talked extensively about what had happened, particularly at night just before he went to sleep. His family continued to be sympathetic and careful listeners. This phase of talking and reflecting on the incident lasted for two to three weeks after the incident. After this, Sahid gradually talked less and less about it, and resumed his normal routines and interests.

Critical Incident Debriefing usually takes place between 24 and 48 hours after the incident and involves a group meeting for all those involved. Exactly who should be involved will depend on the situation. Originally everyone who had been involved, either directly or as a 'helper', would have been included; current thinking suggests that this is not necessarily most effective.

People sit round a table rather than in a circle, to emphasize that this is not a 'therapy group'. Ground rules and guidelines are clarified at the outset. These might include:

- a reminder that people don't have to actively contribute: some people prefer to listen rather than talk
- confidentiality is assured
- the focus is on here and now, although past emotions are likely to emerge
- it is likely that participants may feel worse during or after the debriefing, but this is normal.

Each person is invited to explain how they came to be involved in the event and what role they played in it. After this round of introductions, the debriefing first considers individual expectations and facts, asking questions which specifically relate to the incident experienced:

- What did you expect to happen?
- Did you expect to find . . . (dead bodies/violence/children suffering)?
- What actually happened?

This is followed by an exploration of thoughts and impressions:

- What were your thoughts at first? Later?
- What did you do and why?
- What were your main impressions?
- What really sticks in your memory?
- What did you see/touch/smell/hear/feel?

The next stage is to share emotional reactions:

- What did you feel at first?
- What did you feel later?
- What was the most upsetting thing?
- Did you cry?
- Did you feel angry?
- What happened when you went home?
- How have others treated you since the incident? What have they asked? How have you felt about this?
- What are you feeling now?
- What are you most worried about now?

This is usually the longest part of the debriefing and people may experience strong emotional reactions. The debriefer will move on to the next phase of normalization, during which she or he will emphasize that the reactions and feelings which have been described are normal. An account of the usual reactions to a traumatic incident will be shared, plus symptoms of PTSD. This will include an explanation of how family members may also react.

The group then move on to future planning and long-term coping. Here participants consider how they will access help and support in the short and long-term future from family, friends and/or colleagues:

- What support do you and your family need now?
- Who could offer you this kind of support?

The debriefer will also be able to supply details of helpful organizations and other sources of support. The final stage is disengagement. Any further questions may be asked; plans for future meetings, if necessary, can be made. Participants can also be told what to do if more serious symptoms of PTSD arise – what they might be and where to go for help.

Violent or sudden death

Supporting children who have witnessed or been close to a violent or sudden death, or a suicide, can be especially harrowing for adults. Apart from the normal reactions of grief, the child's fear may be very deep and fantasies about violent death may persist. It is essential to seek professional help if a child is bereaved through suicide, violent death or where the child has witnessed the death or found the body.

Case study

Marie was only 10 years old when her father, Paul, was violently attacked and robbed on the way home from a pub where he had been drinking with friends. Paul, who never regained consciousness, was pronounced dead on arrival at hospital. The perpetrators were never found and the case remains open.

In the weeks that followed, Marie had frequent fantasies, accompanied by vivid images, about the attack itself. She repeatedly replayed in her mind a scene where she imagined her father in great anguish dying alone on the pavement. She constantly reproached herself for not being there to comfort him. She was also tormented by thoughts that in some way Paul was to blame for the attack, imagining that he had been part of a criminal gang or involved in drug dealing. There was nothing to support her suspicions; rather, all the evidence indicated that it was a random attack provoked by the fact that Paul was walking late at night, alone, slightly drunk in a deserted inner-city neighbourhood.

Marie's grief for her father was complicated by the symptoms of post-traumatic stress disorder (PTSD) arising from the suddenness of the death and its violent nature. It was impossible for Marie to begin to work through the normal grieving process until her family had sought help from a specialist.

In such circumstances, the traumatic aspects of the event must be separated from the normal grieving process. The post-traumatic stress reactions – such as when the child, like Marie, has panic attacks, disturbing flashbacks or nightmares, or intrusive memories of the death – can be dealt with through short-term therapeutic intervention. This aspect of the death needs specialist attention since the child is likely to be haunted by images based on the horrific nature of the death. A longer-term goal for intervention by Marie's therapist was to help her to make sense of an essentially random attack and to find some meaning not only in the way that Paul met his death but also in the way he conducted his life as a whole. An important task was to help Marie remember her father as a significant person to her and in his own right, rather than to concentrate on the last minutes of his life.

Seeking professional help should be done as soon as possible after such a bereavement, or whenever the signs and symptoms of distress go beyond the normal grieving process; see Table 2.1 in Chapter 2 for a list of common symptoms of PTSD. This does not mean, however, that adults other than professionals do not have a crucial role to play in supporting the young person at such a time. Despite the trauma of witnessing a violent death, children can show surprising levels of resilience which can be greatly enhanced by helpful, trusted adults through the provision of an essential support network. As we see in Chapter 5 (Peer Support), peers can be an invaluable source of comfort to young people trauma-tized by war (Demetriades, 1996). Dyregrov (1991) writes that children often identify with the helpers rather than with the perpetrator of the violent act.

Studies of children in war zones also give an unexpected perspective. Cairns (1994) reviewed empirical studies of children in war-torn countries where experiences of violence and death are almost commonplace. He argues that, contrary to expectation, children show surprising capacity to adapt to the most adverse circumstances. Without underestimating the adverse effects on children of continuous exposure to violence and danger, Cairns notes that political ideology not only gives children a focus for understanding the reasons underlying the violence but also acts as a protective factor against the emotional stresses of witnessing it. The group aspects of political conflict in a country like Palestine establish feelings of solidarity which can protect individual children against stress. For an excellent review of research on the psychological effects of violence and disaster in both adults and children, including siblings who have witnessed or undergone such experiences, see Newman et al. (1997).

The suicide of a parent

Suicide is an extremely difficult concept for both adults and children to understand. The danger is that the child feels that they were abandoned, unloved, or that they were bad and so caused the death. This is especially the case when the child finds the body. Here it is essential to create opportunities to talk about the disturbing emotions elicited by the event, including thoughts and fantasies around the mode of dying, and the method and the instruments used. Since suicide is often violent, adults tend to protect the child from the true information in a mistaken wish to be helpful. The fact is the child is then more likely to hear so-called 'details' from another, less accurate source, or to understand at some level that there is a family secret which must not be mentioned. The outcome is likely to be that, on top of the loss, the child also has to cope with overwhelming feelings of guilt, anger, and self-reproach. At a profound level, the suicide of a parent affects the very essence of the parent–child relationship and cuts to the heart of the young person's sense of security. Acceptance of the fact of suicide will be hard for the family to bear. Furthermore, there is some evidence that adolescents related to a loved one who has committed suicide are at greater risk of committing suicide themselves (Valente et al., 1988). Dyregrov recommends that adults be aware of behaviour which may signal suicidal intentions on the part of a young person bereaved in this way (adapted from Dyregrov, 1991, pp. 41–2):

- the young person is preoccupied with themes of death
- the young person does final acts like giving away prized possessions
- there is an appearance of peace and contentment following a period of turmoil, signalling that a decision has been made
- sudden changes in eating habits
- withdrawal from friends and family
- changes in sleeping patterns
- persistent feelings of guilt
- making a will
- change in school performance.

Resilience

In this chapter we have addressed some of the ways in which adults and peers can help children deal with the grief of losing someone through death. But we must not forget the inner resources of resilience which children also possess within themselves (see also Chapter 9 on resilience and coping). Some children are better able to cope than others, but research and clinical practice evidences that the majority of children 'come through' a traumatic life event. The issue is further complicated by the fact that some of those children who appear to be coping may have unresolved issues which surface later on in life.

What are the protective factors which act as a support to children and young people faced with a tragic loss? We can categorize these factors of resilience in a cluster: the temperament of the child; the cohesiveness of the family; and the network of supportive agencies in the community, including the peer group. Rutter (1994) argues that the promotion of resilience lies in part in the capacity of the young person to face up to the stress rather than to avoid it. Clearly, where a death is involved the child cannot be expected to do this alone, so the support of family and friends is particularly vital at such a time; but the personal strength of the child is also essential and it is important to take time to acknowledge the courage of the bereaved young person in dealing with loss. The personal qualities most associated with resilience are: positive reappraisal; guidance; support; a problem-solving approach; and less reliance on resigned acceptance (Frydenberg, 1997).

The classic study by Freud and Dann (1951) provides moving evidence of the power of the peer group to buffer children from the most grievous losses and deprivations. Six children who lost their parents as babies during the Holocaust remained together in a concentration camp and for a period afterwards, during rehabilitation in the therapeutic nursery run by Anna Freud and her colleagues. These individuals, now middle-aged, are still in contact with one another, and it is believed that a crucial factor in protecting them from mental and physical breakdown was the support of the tightly-knit peer group.

Children cannot be categorized into those who cope and those who do not cope with bereavement. They respond in a whole range of ways across a continuum and over time. Resilience is not a discrete characteristic but one which varies with the age and the circumstances of the child. A sensitive awareness is needed so that at each stage of development children express their feelings differently. Adults must be ready to offer help but should never underestimate the capacity which children have to recover from even the most traumatic event.

4

STORYTELLING AND EVERYDAY CHAT

My early experiences teaching children convinced me that to get to know a child you must listen attentively to her stories and invite her to tell you more. It is remarkable how complex and dense with meaning a young child's story can be, filled with intriguing clues for the psychological investigator and at the same time appearing so simple, organic and spontaneous ... The key is to delve into children's narratives for information and meaning without losing one's appreciation for their beauty and communicative force – to learn how to look at them closely but still really listen to them.

(Engel, 1995, pp. viii–ix)

The power of narrative

As we have seen, it is possible to support young people in finding solutions to their difficulties in a whole range of different arenas – within the family, in school, and through networks in the community. The key point is that adults may not need to do extraordinary things to be supportive. In fact, adults are given many everyday opportunities which, if used constructively, can help young people to make the most of the resources they have to hand. Throughout history and across cultures we find recurring evidence of the power of narrative to heal.

Children and young people naturally use play, drawing and story to work through stressful situations – to analyse, to sort out, to understand. The tradition of storytelling and drama allows communities of people to tell and retell significant events, describing and sharing the coping strategies employed and thereby educating the listeners. Creative therapies – using art, music and drama – draw upon imagery and metaphor to provide a safe environment within which to explore painful memories and to create new futures. In this chapter we consider some of the creative approaches which can be employed to help children and young people work through and come to terms with problematic situations and relationships. Most importantly, we want to emphasize the value of ordinary talk, drawing and play as strong vehicles for working with children and young people in distress.

Bruner (1990) suggests that narrative form plays a key part in the development of children's capacity to make sense of events in their lives and to evoke meanings. Scarlett and Wolf (1979), observing children's storytelling through the enactment of scenes using model figures, showed that whereas children under the age of 3 years demonstrate play which is mainly carried out by actions, by the time children are ready to enter first school the meaning of their stories is much more likely to be expressed in linguistic ways – through sequences of events, through the dialogue of characters in a story, and through communications which reveal a growing sense of audience; later, these narratives can be captured in written form. The process continues with school-age children as they demonstrate social awareness, the capacity to see the world through the eyes of an invented character, and the ability to express empathy for the feelings of people in imagined settings (Engel, 1995).

Parents play an important part in helping the child to develop as a narrator when they encourage talk, fantasy play and drawing. They can also read fiction and non-fiction with the child, so helping to enrich the world of the imagination. Perhaps the most important role of the adult lies in the capacity to listen to what children have to say. This can be a significant way of entering into the inner world of the child and allows an opportunity to respond to any themes of anxiety or fear which may arise by exploring multiple perspectives on a theme.

Drama and role-play

Drama and role-play have great potential for helping children and young people to gain an understanding of their own lives, to rehearse different solutions and strategies, to explore the hypothetical and possible, to learn about how other people think and feel, and to work constructively with disturbing emotions like anger, fear and hate. Not only does this learning take place within the safety of a playful situation, but also there are other people involved in the process, whether as participants or as onlookers. Whereas many children and young people may find it difficult to talk about or describe their concerns and anxieties, they can demonstrate and explore the dilemmas they face through role-play. As Dwivedi (1993) writes, when describing group work with adolescents:

> Total reliance on talking . . . can be too taxing and difficult to maintain. As the youngsters, particularly those with a degree of disturbance, become bored, excitable, demanding, over-anxious, avoidant, restless or agitated, words alone may be unable to contain the energy of the group. . . . Role playing, psychodrama, Gestalt techniques, video-taping and playing back, watching films and so forth, similarly provide alternative perspectives and an increased capacity to focus on relevant matters. (p. 34–35)

Role-play and role-taking can be seen in the earliest stages of play. Pre-school children will often take roles which reflect familiar everyday experiences. They will act out exchanges between themselves and family members, scenes from playgroup or nursery, from the supermarket and so on. They can also be observed to explore less familiar situations through the medium of role-play. Role-play enables them to venture into the world of fantasy and make-believe as they enact monsters, witches and princesses. But it is also rooted in reality. Children and often adults continue to observe their own lives as a series of episodes with a 'text' and actors, supporting cast and an ending. The skills of role-taking and empathy develop throughout childhood and can be charted in the continuing interest in creating imaginative stories. Through characters and events, children at primary school and beyond continue to experiment with roles and explore new situations imaginatively. This helps us to become socially aware. Even as adults we often re-enact problematic situations we have encountered during our day, replaying the situation and including alternative statements or actions – the things we would like to have said.

Drama teachers (Jennings, 1986) believe that we do not grow out of role-play but can continue to respond to situations which give us the opportunity to empathize with the feelings of another person, explore the outcomes of our actions, experience what it might be like to be treated in certain ways, and get feedback from others in role as we act out a range of emotions. Furthermore, since drama engages the emotions, it is a method which is likely to be motivating and enjoyable.

When using role-play and drama to work with children and young people we are not concerned with performing a play but rather with exploring and responding to ideas about relationships. The teacher is firmly 'at the helm' and, as the children engage in roles, she or he stands back from the situation in order to observe, reflect and interpret the interactions which are taking place. Re-enactments of difficult situations encountered by a child or young person which involve the focus child as director and onlooker also enable the child to take this more objective view. When the young person actually observes his or her situation enacted, he or she can also often identify the solution. At other times the teacher may be more actively involved in the role-playing exercises in order to model the activity and illustrate possible responses. Theatre techniques may also be helpful – especially if the participants are anxious about taking an active role themselves. In theatre, the youngsters watch an enactment as a dramatic performance; the action can be stopped at particular points to enable discussion of thoughts, feelings, motivations, and possible next steps and their consequences. The audience can advise the actors and then see the consequences of their advice within the ensuing scenes.

Dramatherapy and psychodrama are more therapeutic uses of the role-play medium. Conn (1997) describes the successful use of dramatherapy to work with children and young people who experience emotional and behavioural difficulties in schools. She points out that typical school responses to 'acting out' behaviour is to discuss, remonstrate and/or apply sanctions. However, 'acting out' is, as the name suggests, a dramatic expression and therefore is more creatively explored through the dramatic medium. Conn argues that the image of the fighter is strong with many aggressive children and she works with them to move from the 'bad' or criminal image to the dignified, honourable and controlled image – the warrior or guardian. She writes:

> By working poetically and ritualistically, the 'fighter' in these children can be converted from something that is chaotic and bleak into something much more estimable and useful. (1997, p. 15)

Stories and narrative

Literature is a powerful medium for addressing important personal issues. Protherough (1983) argues that stories which we shape around our own lives arise out of our accumulated responses to real events and to those we experience in imaginative fiction. 'The actual and the fictional are inseparably interlocked within us' (Protherough, 1983, p. 15). Protherough found young readers reported that they often imagined they were one of the characters or were in the places where the events of the story took place. Some reported that they were trying to make links between the world of the book and their own life experiences. The reader's values and experiences interact with those portrayed in the story; the themes of most literature are those of life: relationships, conflict, love, betrayal, death, danger, childhood, adolescence, adulthood. Literature helps us to understand we are not alone in our experiences and to learn about the impact of similar life events on the characters within the text – their emotions, their thoughts, their actions.

Guggenbhul (1991) suggested the symbolic images of fantasy can help children to work through emotional conflicts. The themes of the imagination are real because they deal with real emotional issues in the child's life and give children the opportunity to resolve inner conflicts. The emphasis in this type of work is on allowing pupils to listen to stories which describe situations or problems which are universal. They are encouraged to supplement the story with their own fantasies – by making up new episodes or by enhancing a scene. Once the story has been told, the pupils explore the images evoked by the story through art or drama. Often the pictures or role-plays produced by the children relate to their own lives and situations. The teacher helps pupils to do this by discussing the emotions and meanings portrayed in their work with them. Group discussion draws out parallels between the story, the images elicited through the art or drama, and the conflicts faced by the children themselves. Through the discussion, the pupils move from the imaginary to the real and are then able to apply the lessons learnt from fiction to their own lives.

Hardy (1977, p. 14) states that narrative is the 'continuation of the remembering, dreaming and planning that is in life imposed on the uncertain, attenuated, interrupted and unpredictable or meaningless flow of happenings'. She sees narrative as a fundamental way of organizing experience which is part of everyone's life. Like Applebee (1978) and Britton (1977), she claims that narrative mediates between the person's individual needs and the constraints of reality. This approach to narrative confirms the self-reports of children yet avoids the extremes of focusing too heavily on deep-seated emotional conflicts in the child.

From this perspective readers are themselves constructing and reconstructing the story which they read or hear. No two individuals will re-create the story in exactly the same way. Meaning is something which emerges through the reader's emotional interaction with the text.

As with drama and role-play, story and narrative can be used generally to enable children and young people to explore concerns, broaden their understanding of life dilemmas and how to cope with them, or can be used more therapeutically. Benson (1995) uses metaphor to work with young children. Her work is based on the use of hypnosis as a therapeutic medium. She has noted that hypnotic or 'trance' states often occur spontaneously within contexts where our attention is narrowed or focused, and which also involve repetitive stimuli and imaginative involvement. For young children, listening to a story combines these elements. Once children become engrossed in a story and are in this trance state, positive messages about how to cope with difficulties they are encountering can be introduced via the actions of the hero or heroine. Benson recommends that the person working with the child makes up a story which mirrors the child's own situation and which includes a metaphor for the child which she or he will be interested in. The child can be involved in modifying the story or continuing it as a serial – using it to express his or her feelings or concerns. The role of the adult is to demonstrate effective coping strategies through the actions and responses of the metaphor (see page 68 for case study example).

Enid MacNeill (unpublished), a psychologist in Sheffield, has developed an approach for helping children and young people talk about themselves and their concerns. This approach accepts that sometimes it is easier to talk to someone else about sensitive matters if you do not have to look at them. MacNeill uses drawing as a tool for encouraging conversation. She starts off with a blank piece of paper and draws a rough sketch of the child or young person as she sees him or her. As she does this she sits alongside the young person, comments on what she is seeing and encourages them to tell her what other things she should draw. This may be about family, friends, a current situation and so on. Together they create a visual map of what is going on in the child or young person's life. By working together on a practical activity, she finds that children and young people are able to talk more openly about what is going on in their lives.

Case study

Jim is a 7-year-old boy who is very aggressive at school and at home. He lashes out and throws objects. His parents are separated and although Jim would like to live with his mother, she doesn't want him to live with her because of his violence. His father has beaten him very badly on a number of occasions. Jim loves motorbikes. The following story was used to work with him on his behaviour in school.

This is a story about a fantastic motorbike. It is a young motorbike with a strong engine. It goes so fast that people stop and look in amazement as it zooms past, admiring its beautiful paintwork and smooth lines. The motorbike, which we will call Zoom [name chosen by Jim], still lives in the factory where it was made. The owner of the factory loves the little motorbike and looks after it well, polishing its paintwork until it gleams, keeping it full of oil and fuel. He made the bike and he's so proud of its strength and speed and beauty. The bike has another owner too but the other owner lives in a different factory. The bike would like to stay with the other owner and gets angry and sad about this sometimes. When Zoom gets angry and sad, he revs up his engines and frightens the other bikes. He rears up on his back wheel and charges into the other bikes and people. The other bikes are scared of Zoom when he does this. The owner gets terribly cross with Zoom when this happens, and sometimes he has hit Zoom with a spanner and damaged his beautiful paintwork. The owner is always terribly sorry when he has calmed down but it's scary for everyone when both the owner and Zoom are in a rage.

Every day the bike goes to the garage, to learn how to drive safely and well. Sometimes Zoom comes into the garage cross and mad. He revs his engine at the other bikes, he charges into them and scares them away. The mechanics shout at him when he does this and then he feels even madder and revs his engine even louder. When he's calmer he still feels sad because none of the other bikes will play with him – they're too scared.

One day a new mechanic came to the garage. He saw Zoom in the corner of the forecourt, looking cross and sad and alone.

'Hey, Zoom', he said. Zoom growled and revved his engine but the mechanic just stayed calm and quiet.

'Zoom, you look pretty miserable to me, mate . . . things don't look very good . . . let's think about how we can make this better.'

'Hmph', muttered Zoom.

'I bet if you kept your engine purring gently it would make you feel calmer and the other bikes wouldn't be so scared of you. You wouldn't get told off by the other mechanics so much either. You're a smashing bike and I bet you could teach some of the other bikes how to drive well and safely – they would love to be able to drive like you.'

'Hmph', muttered Zoom.

'You think about it . . . I bet you can do it.'

The new mechanic wandered off to the engine room. Zoom thought about what he had said. At that moment a little bike whizzed past near Zoom. Zoom calmed his engine and purred gently.

'Hi, Zoom', said the little bike.

'Hi', said Zoom, 'Your engine sounds good today.'

'Yeah, the mechanic did some work on it and I've been practising driving smoothly.'

'Well, I find that if I control the fuel flow smoothly that really helps.'

'Oh thanks, Zoom. Hey, Zoom, you know that fantastic wheely trick you do . . .'

'D'you want me to show you?'

'Yeah!!!'

As Zoom began to show all the good tricks he could do, keeping his engine purring gently the other bikes in the forecourt began to gather round and watch.

'That's great, Zoom.'

'Cor, Zoom, you're the best!'

Zoom felt great, his engine purred with happiness. The other bikes let him join in with their games and practising; the mechanics praised his work.

When the owner of the factory came to collect him he was thrilled; he said, 'Well done, Zoom, well done.'

Metaphors in the story with which Jim readily identified included: Zoom – Jim; Factory owners – parents; Garage – school; Mechanics – teachers; New mechanic – therapist; Other bikes – peers.

Very soon Jim began to add to the story, weaving into it issues he identified as important in his life and exploring the possible impact of his behaviour on others through the bike metaphor. He was initially interested in the bike doing outrageous things such as running people over. When he did this sort of thing the storyteller brought in the consequences of his actions and encouraged Jim to think of ways of avoiding that situation or of resolving conflict. While this work was going on, Jim's teachers found his behaviour gradually changing. Jim adopted some of the more constructive behaviours demonstrated by Zoom. His teacher began to use the story with him, often to explore situations that had gone well as well as situations that had been problematic. The metaphor offered Jim a safe way to explore his behaviour and his life with concerned adults.

Television and film

Although modern TV and film sometimes get a bad press for encouraging aggression and romanticizing sex (Strasburger, 1995), they have become the modern version of storytelling. This is particularly the case with soap operas, which present dilemr and explore solutions – some of which are more effective than others. The drama for soaps, plays and films often centres round a critical incident or a difficult relationship. Consequently they offer opportunities for relating what is happening on the screen to what is happening in the youngster's life. Selecting a plot which is similar to the events in the child's life can lead to joint watching and discussion of differences, similarities; effective and ineffective coping strategies; and the emotional reactions of the actors and of the child.

Art and music

Both art and music provide a means for communicating without speaking. In therapeutic art groups, a small group of children will be brought together on a regular basis for six months or a year. Within the art therapy room there are a wide array of materials which each child can use freely during the session to create their piece of artwork. The art therapists use discussion which arises spontaneously within the group and during reflection time to explore themes and issues which emerge through the art work. Dalley (1993) has found that these art therapy groups are particularly helpful for youngsters experiencing difficulties with peer relationships, or aggressive or disruptive behaviour.

Music can be used similarly. The therapist and the child can also have a 'conversation' using instruments, with the therapist beginning by echoing the child's tune or beat in order to set up a repricocity. It is also possible to listen to music and then explore the emotions inspired by or represented through it.

5

PEER SUPPORT

'Someone should talk to them and reassure them and cheer them up really, 'cause when they're upset the bullies will sort of see that,' said Paul, aged 14.

(MacLeod and Morris, 1996, p. 85)

'It was a boy . . . he was new and he never got round to making friends . . . People were basically testing him out to see if he was scared or to see if he was strong, and just what happened is he didn't jump straight on the person, so he was getting bullied. A teacher was holding him. I passed by and saw him very upset and I was concerned, so I went over there to talk to him. I knew the teacher quite well, and she knew me, and then she asked me if I could help. So, from then, I got him referred and I took him through the procedure of confidentiality, and told him how to sort out his problem and what he can do. From then on I've actually been noticed. He says, "Hello" to me, I say, "Hello" to him. He said, "Thank you", and he's got plenty of friends now.'

(Sean, a peer supporter, aged 14)

The importance of friendships

Most young people say that they would like to act in a cooperative, friendly way towards one another. It is not always enough, however, to rely on this natural willingness to help a peer in distress since there can also be strong pressures to deny help to those who are most in need (the next section deals with these conflicting pressures in relation to bullying). There may be fear of retaliation, lack of confidence, anxiety about being rebuffed, unwillingness to take an emotional risk, concern that the right words or actions may not emerge, or a basic lack of social skill. Peer support systems offer structures and training which ensure that the help is there when it is most needed. These systems appear in a variety of forms in schools today, including befriending and counselling-based peer support. In this chapter, by looking at systems which work through the relationship with a peer to offer support to children in need, we overview how they work and how useful they are both to those in need and to those who offer help. We look in turn at befriending, Circles of Friends, mediation/conflict resolution and peer 'counselling-based' support; their general impact on the school's emotional climate and the development in young people of a sense of citizenship and responsibility are also discussed. As you read, think back to the issues discussed in Chapter 1, exploring the basic rights to which children are entitled.

Peer relationships are of critical importance to young people; it is through these interactions that so much can be learned about self, others and the social world. Being close to someone, sharing experiences, having disagreements and resolving differences are all part of growing up. If these experiences of peer relationships are, on balance, good ones, the child grows up with a positive outlook on life and the expectation of being liked and valued by those who matter to him or her. The young person also gains invaluable opportunities to take the perspective of others – try to see things their way. But if the experiences are less favourable, the long-term outlook for emotional well-being is likely to be bleak. Being among a group of peers who apparently have no difficulty in relating to one another with confidence and enjoyment can be immensely dispiriting and undermining to the child who is often ignored and deliberately left out, or who is derided or rejected. Here are some common answers which young people gave to the question, 'Why are friends important to you?':

- We share things.
- I can talk to her about my feelings.
- When my dog died and I was upset he helped me.
- It is fun to be in her company.
- We have lots of laughs.
- We teach each other to do things like games.
- We look out for each other. He protects me and I protect him.
- We phone each other up for a chat.
- I feel safe when I'm around my friends in lessons and all that, but I find I'm unsafe when I'm by myself – [when] there's not a lot of people around me.

The themes which recur concern closeness and intimacy, mutuality and liking, and learning about power differentials.

Children who find it hard to form close affiliations with their peers (for example, those who are neglected or rejected for whatever reason) may develop behaviour patterns which in turn perpetuate the difficulty. They may become timid and unresponsive in groups; they may have angry outbursts; they may become provocative and attention-seeking; they may develop a downcast demeanour which distances them from others. In each case, the long-term effects can persist well into adult life.

Dealing with bullying behaviour: bystanding or standing by

Another crucial aspect of social relationships concerns *power*. We cannot dispute the existence of power differentials in social groups. Some children are more talented, stronger, more expert or more fun to be with than others. It is important during development that children and young people learn to affirm their own and others' strengths and weaknesses and to acknowledge the richness which diversity and difference have to offer. Problems arise, however, when that power differential is abused – for example, when the stronger person uses their strength to intimidate or put down a peer, or promotes their own interests at the expense of others. This kind of behaviour is broadly defined as bullying and is a major source of emotional distress among young people. It is a complex social phenomenon involving onlookers and bystanders as well as bullies and victims.

Surveys of children's perspectives on bullying (see, for example, MacLeod and Morris, 1996) show that most children dislike it and that a teacher can count on the majority of children in a class to be opposed to it. But paradoxically – researchers such as Rigby and Slee (1991) in Australia; Menesini et al. (1996) in Italy; Morita (1996) in Japan; and Eslea and Smith (1996) in the UK – have all found that bullies can usually find allies who despise weaker or more helpless peers. Those who are 'non-committal' – the bystanders – can also be perceived by the victims as acting in collusion with the bullies. Pepler's (1996) observational studies on Toronto school playgrounds provide supportive evidence that bullying is indeed a social event and that this social context has a powerful influence on whether bystanders act responsibly or remain 'neutral'. She found that peers were present in 85 per cent of the bullying episodes in both the playground and the classroom and that peers adopted a number of roles: co-bullies, supporters, audience and 'seldom intervenors'.

Salmivalli et al. (1996) argue that it is possible to assign a participant role to 87 per cent of the pupils present at a bullying episode. The most common of these participant roles are 'assistant', 'reinforcer', 'outsider', and 'defender'. *Assistants* join in the bullying, though they do not instigate it; they help the bully by, for example, holding the victim down. *Reinforcers* act as audience to the bullying incident, laugh at the victim and incite the bully to do more. They are likely to be excited by the incident and to call others over to view the fun with comments like, 'Come on over. There's a fight! Someone's being done!' They take overt pleasure in the distress of their peer. *Outsiders* stay outside the situation, remain inactive and pretend not to notice what is happening. Typically when they see a peer in distress they think or say to themselves: 'I'm all right and that's all that matters' or 'it's none of my business'. They are likely to claim that they know nothing of the person's unhappiness and so remain, as they see it, neutral; they are unaware that, by their inaction, they appear to the victim to be colluding with the actions of the bullies. *Defenders* comfort the victim, tell an adult about what is happening, or even attack the bully; they may also go out of their way to be friends with the victim afterwards and encourage the victim to seek help in some way. They are more likely to confront the bullies and the re-inforcers by asking them to stop or by running to get others to help stop the harassment. After the incident, they are the ones who will stay behind to comfort and support the victim. It is they who will encourage the victim to tell an adult; they may well also promise to keep the victim company and devise ways of making sure that the victim is safe.

Salmivalli et al. noted that boys are more likely to be actively involved in the bullying process and their most frequent participant roles are those of assistant and reinforcer. By contrast, girls are most commonly found in the roles of outsider and defender. Salmivalli et al. recommend that anti-bullying interventions should be directed at the whole peer group and not only at the bullies and their victims.

The discrepancy between what children say and what they actually do when faced with a bullying situation suggests that there are conflicts taking place within them, with implications for their emotional well-being as well as for that of the more active participants. Hazler (1996) argues that bystanders fail to take action for one of the following basic reasons:

- they do not know what to do
- they are fearful of becoming the brunt of the bullies' attacks
- they might do the wrong thing which could cause even more problems.

The safest line of action in these circumstances is likely to be non-intervention. But this avoidance of involvement on the part of a bystander has its own form of anguish.

To illustrate the point, we quote an American researcher as he recalls the merciless bullying of a classmate, thirty years after the event. Diane joined his class in the sixth grade as a newcomer from another school. She was overweight, was slightly below average in her studies, and suffered from acne; yet, in his words, 'no single characteristic rendered her grossly different from the rest of us'. Soon after she joined the class she was nicknamed 'Boxer', after a cartoon hound, and the campaign had begun. She suffered teasing, verbal harassment, poking, tripping and pinching. Ink blots appeared on her school work. One particular incident stands out:

> While Miss Torgerson drank coffee in the teachers' lounge one day during the hectic weeks leading up to Christmas, Dave sneaked up behind Diane's desk, where she slouched, endeavouring to remain unnoticed. He generated a ripping noise that echoed through the room. He shouted to the existing silence, 'God damn, Boxer, did you fart again?' Mocking laughter and dog barks rose up in the room.
> Diane's face reddened. She rose so abruptly that Dave put up his hands as if to protect his face or square off for fisticuffs. She ran out of the room, crying and screaming unintelligibly. Her strangled voice came out in sobs, frighteningly adult in their anguish. I had never experienced such hopeless, deeply felt grief in someone my own age.
> Our treatment of Diane was literally torture. I despised myself for not intervening. I longed to have the adults in my life help me make sense of the situation and my feelings about it. I wanted some force to swoop down and fix Diane's predicament. Perhaps simple-mindedly, I hoped the primary perpetrators would be brought to justice. (Hoover, 1996, p. 11)

Hoover's inaction may have temporarily reduced his fear about being personally attacked or ridiculed by the bullies and their supporters; he may even have convinced himself that it would only have caused her further distress to come to her rescue. Yet this account demonstrates the inner turmoil experienced by a bystander who would have liked to intervene but who lacked the courage or skill to contravene the powerful norms of the peer group. Sadly for Diane, she could not have known that at least some classmates were appalled at the treatment meted out to her.

Hazler (1996) confirms this view that inaction can give bystanders a sense of powerlessness similar to that being experienced by the victim. The victim's loss of self-esteem among the peer group is clear to perpetrators and to those who play a less active part. But the consequences for bystanders, he argues, are also negative:

> An adrenalin rush may well come with watching someone be victimised, but there is no pride or self-respect in knowing you are an ineffective bystander in someone else's tragic situation. Regaining the self-respect and confidence that goes with feeling in control does not have to come by accident. It can also be conscientiously fostered by counselors, educators, and parents. (Hazler, 1996, p. 15)

There are longer-term consequences arising from the failure to take action when faced with a peer in distress. Many young people become desensitized to others' suffering the longer they are exposed to situations where intervention does not take place (Safran and Safran, 1985).

It seems likely that adults wishing to initiate peer-led interventions to combat bullying will turn to defenders, the young people who spontaneously 'stand by' the victim rather than 'bystand', for assistance. The interventions which we describe in the following sections describe the active part which adults can play in building on this potential for help and providing the training, guidance and supervision which can channel it into effective action to help children and young people who are at risk because:

- they are strangers from another school or from another culture
- they have had traumatic experiences which distance them from their peers
- they have a physical or learning disability
- they are going through a troubling life event, for example separation or loss in the family
- they have acquired inappropriate ways of behaving towards their peers and are consequently rejected or isolated
- they have been involved in bullying situations.

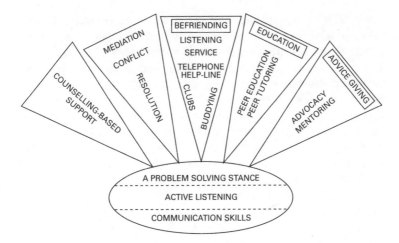

Figure 5.1   *Models of peer support (designed by Don Briggs)*

In all these circumstances, we argue, young people can play an active part in alleviating the distress which arises, not only in the children involved but also in those who are onlookers.

In the following sections we explore a number of forms of peer support, including befriending, Circles of Friends, mediation/conflict resolution, and counselling-based approaches. These models of peer support are represented schematically in Figure 5.1.

Befriending

This approach encompasses a number of forms but is essentially about building on the natural helping skills which children learn through the processes of everyday life and interactions with friends and in the family. In some cases, this help is of a purely practical nature. Konet (1991) and Demetriades (1996) describe the value of after-school clubs where students as befrienders offer companionship, activities and refreshments to peers who would otherwise be miserable and alone. Such systems may not require intensive training, simply the presence of friendly young people with a willingness to help others. To a vulnerable child, the existence of this system, run by friendly, supportive peers, can offer an essential lifeline.

Carr (1994) counted over thirty terms to describe the role, with the most common being buddy, befriender, peer helper or peer partner. But the essential basis of this approach concerns active listening, a caring attitude and a practical approach to the issue. Here are some examples. Kaye and Webb (1996) describe a system through which sixth formers were given personal responsibility for small groups of pupils new to the school. In their groups, they facilitated discussion around issues such as feelings of loneliness, making friends, dealing with bullying behaviour, learning to share, and so on. The well-being of the younger students was enhanced and the helpers gained also through increased confidence and a belief in their own efficacy. Bourgault (1991) also trained senior students in active listening, assertiveness and leadership; they were then ready to implement helpful interventions to support students new to the school by facilitating small group discussion of issues like managing homework, coping with peer group pressure and becoming aware of their sexuality. There were immediate and long-term effects which were beneficial to both younger students and peer helpers.

James and her colleagues (1991) trained 16- to 17-year-old secondary school students to use basic listening skills, to be aware of the impact of facial expression and body language on others, to use open questions, to give sympathetic responses and to learn to tolerate silence. Each helper was then matched with a younger student with learning difficulties, some of whom also had interpersonal problems. The peer befrienders' brief was to listen attentively to the younger peers and show an interest in the issues they raised. The befriending was not designed to be a substitute for academic tutoring but rather to complement it. Sessions took place informally in the library, in the art room and on the playing fields; the meetings had, as a starting point, an area of shared interest such as pottery. When the younger children expressed negative feelings about themselves (for example, 'I am hopeless at spelling'), the befriender was trained to respond in a supportive way – perhaps describing something which he or she had found hard, showing empathy for the peer's feelings, and emphasizing the part which the younger child could play in working towards change. Both experimental and control groups received specialist academic tuition from teachers, but the ones who had been paired with a befriender as well demonstrated significant and lasting gains in reading and spelling in comparison with the controls. In addition, there were marked changes in attitudes to study, self-confidence and social interaction.

There is evidence that peer helpers have the potential to help young people in the midst of very difficult life experiences.

Demetriades (1996) showed that peer partners, in the setting of an after-school club, were able to offer effective support to young people who had been severely traumatized by war, had experienced the loss of close family relationships and were trying to rebuild their lives in a strange country. She points out that peer support did not replace professional intervention, but it did provide a crucial emotional and social safety net for very vulnerable young people. It is significant that many of those who were helped, in turn, became peer partners in the scheme.

Quarmby (1993) has also shown the supportive role that may be played by peers in helping adolescents cope with bereavement, as part of a wider system of professional intervention. He set up support groups, lasting six sessions, for bereaved young people. His participants responded well to the experience and were able to express feelings in the groups which they had been unable to share in other settings. The reason they gave was that other group members understood the particular difficulties since they were all suffering from loss of a loved one. Quarmby comments on the 'natural' quality of empathy and active listening which arose spontaneously within the groups.

Circles of Friends

The Circles of Friends approach was developed in Canada and North America, but has recently been introduced into the UK (Newton et al., 1996). The focus is on one child who is presenting behavioural or emotional difficulties in school. The rationale behind this method is that children with difficult behaviour may become alienated from their peer group and so have difficulty in forming close friendships. This, in turn, compounds the problem. Creating a Circle of Friends is an opportunity to break the cycle and instead to give the target child an opportunity to feel and behave in different ways. The power of the peer group is acknowledged and the aim is to mobilize this force to encourage the child to behave in ways which are more acceptable to both adults and members of the peer group, so opening the way to forming genuine relationships with peers. Essentially, the Circle consists of members of the child's class and a key member of staff; the group meets weekly with the following aims:

- to create a support network for the child
- to reduce the child's challenging behaviour

- to enable the child to deal with issues as they arise in everyday situations
- to help the child to understand his or her own behaviour more clearly
- to help the child make friends.

Taylor (1996) recommends the method strongly since helping these children make friends is easy in theory but very hard for adults to achieve; the peer group has a significant part to play here. She suggests that all participants, not only the target child, benefit from being a part of a Circle of Friends, for the following reasons. The children develop empathy for another child who is in some difficulty, and come to understand more deeply why people behave in ways which are not always easy to deal with. They develop a wider vocabulary of emotions; they learn about the importance of listening carefully to one another, and of valuing different perspectives and contributions. The process of being in the Circle gives children the opportunity to think about an issue, to explore it through face-to-face interaction in a safe group, and possibly to resolve some of the difficulties. As a result, their interpersonal skills in general are greatly enhanced since they see the possibility of making changes, experience the processes of change, and observe any outcomes.

Teachers involved in the Circle frequently comment on the benefits and are often surprised by the extent to which the peer group in the circle can demonstrate a caring, thoughtful approach to another child who, in everyday settings, may often have been rejected or neglected.

Mediation and conflict resolution

Peer mediation is more structured than most befriending schemes but, like them, can be adapted to a wide range of school settings (see Chapter 8 for a more detailed account). It is reported to result in a substantial decrease in the incidence of aggressive behaviour (Stacey, 1996). The skills can be learned by pupils from around 9 years of age through to adolescence. The peer mediation method has evolved from the 'no-blame' position which holds that one of the most effective ways of resolving conflict is to create a 'win–win' outcome. One of the problems with many attempts at conflict resolution is that, too often, the outcome is that one wins and the other loses. Common interpersonal and intergroup problems – bullying, racist name-calling, fighting and quarrelling – may well escalate if unresolved; on the other hand, punishing wrongdoers can leave feelings of resentment, and the behaviour may become even more entrenched. Peer mediation, by contrast, offers a non-punitive solution.

How does peer mediation work? Typically, two trained peer mediators work as a team to encourage problem solving between people who are in disagreement. The mediators meet with the disputants; each disputant tells his or her story, expresses how he or she feels about the incident and the mediators listen without passing judgement; disputants are each asked what they would like to happen next; and finally they are all involved in exploring what might be done to ensure that each participant in the dispute comes away from the mediation with a positive 'win–win' feeling and the sense that the outcome is fair to both sides.

The mediation process can be carried out where the dispute occurs – often in the playground. Students receive a highly-structured programme of training which equips them with specific skills for mediating in disputes, including: active listening; the expression of feelings; clarification of meaning through clear, unambiguous terms; appropriate sensitivity to the meaning of non-verbal communication; and different ways of asking questions. A key aspect involves learning how to give 'I' messages owned, by the speaker (for example, 'I am very angry right now' or 'When you said that you hurt my feelings'), rather than vague generalizations such as 'Everyone knows that he is a bully' or 'What do you expect when someone insults you?' Role-play is used a great deal to practice newly-learned skills, such as inter-vening in a playground quarrel which has got out of hand, or mediating between a child who bullies and a child who is victimized.

Counselling-based approaches

In this section, we look at peer support systems more directly modelled on a counselling approach. As with befriending approaches, these vary widely in emphasis, encompassing issues like bullying, loneliness, adjusting to a new school, and dealing with separation and loss. But there are some common elements in these counselling-based programmes of support, including the teaching of basic skills of active listening, empathy, problem solving and supportiveness. First, they involve a direct response to a request for help with regard to a specific problem. They are generally implemented through a formal system of referral soon after the request for help has occurred. Second, they all involve giving the peer helpers skills and strategies for enabling the young people involved in the situation to find a resolution to the problem. Third, though the direct action is taken by the peer helpers, adults retain a supportive and supervisory role without imposing solutions. Fourth, they are non-punitive interventions which do not seek to apportion blame but to offer clear and genuine channels of communication among those involved in the situation. Counselling-based interventions of this kind recognize that pupils have potential to assume a helpful role in tackling a problem.

In terms of implementation, they all require specialist training for both staff and pupils. All take place outside the classroom and so depend on the school having the resources and commitment to facilitate the peer support system. Typically the system will be coordinated by a member of staff with particular personal qualities of dedication and commitment, often in partnership with a professional linked to the school and with specialist training in counselling or psychotherapy. Opposite is one account of the process of selection and training in an 11 to 16 age range comprehensive school.

Training must take account of the specific requirements of the school and most manuals of training recommend that practitioners adapt the guidelines to their own setting. Typically, the training guides (for example, Carr and Saunders, 1980; Cowie and Sharp, 1996) incorporate ideas and exercises from a range of sources, including role-play, video work, lectures, group work, opportunities in pairs or threes to work on trainees' own issues, and self-awareness activities. Manuals generally recommend that training should be not less than thirty hours but, in reality, this varies greatly in schemes which are currently running. The training may take place intensively or in once-a-week sessions. The extent and quality of the training depends, it is clear, on the availability of qualified staff and the supportiveness of the senior management in the school.

Once training has taken place, students are regularly supervised in their work and have follow-up sessions to review special issues as they arise. This, in turn, will often lead to requests for further training. In all cases it is recommended that training should be experiential, whatever the orientation of the trainers may be. The most effective training seems to be that which gives trainees the

Case study

Prior to the introduction of the peer support programme Mrs Y, the coordinating teacher, presented the idea of training in peer support to parents, pupils and teachers. The opportunity to take part in training was open to pupils in Years 8, 9 and 10; interested pupils were asked to complete an application form and CV, a short list was selected and from that list applicants were interviewed by Mrs Y. Finally nine pupils were selected for training.

Peer supporters participated in sixteen hours of training conducted by an external facilitator, trained and experienced as a counsellor. During the training, the leader introduced basic listening skills, empathy, responsiveness to others' feelings, the development of a vocabulary of feelings, and a problem-solving approach to personal and social issues; she modelled the approach in all her interactions with the pupils. The peer supporters were given a room in which to see pupils during the lunch hour, and a secure filing cabinet for confidential records. Mrs Y and two other staff were also trained in the method; their training took place over two half-days.

The peer helpers were monitored, given feedback, and helped to resolve the problems they encountered in the course of ongoing supervision by Mrs Y and her colleagues. Each week they met with the peer helpers to discuss the issues they had encountered and to offer support and guidance as appropriate. During the autumn term, weekly supervision was also offered by the external facilitator. On the basis of these supervision sessions, four further training workshops were given.

---

opportunity to share their own experiences, and to practise the skills of listening and responding appropriately in a safe environment; training is also most effective when delivered by adults who model good practice and a sensitive awareness of young people's issues.

Evaluating peer support

Evaluations of this kind of intervention are difficult in the short term since researchers have to wait until the system has been in place for some time before the effects are fully evident. To add to the researcher's difficulties, schools differ widely in their perceptions and experiences of the issues, so there is a tendency for methods of application of the peer support method to change over time as peers and adults adapt the intervention to suit their particular needs. Since the evidence tends to be based on case studies, it is likely to take time before enough material has been gathered to supply convincing evidence. There are additional problems in that the peer supporters are bound by a code of ethics covering the issue of confidentiality, and the recipients of help may be reluctant to be interviewed about their experiences of support.

The benefits

Despite the practical constraints, research in the field of peer support (Carr, 1994; Cowie and Sharp, 1996; Smith et al., 1994) indicates that these systems have benefits for the helpers as well as those in need of help: they enable young people who would otherwise be bystanders to take responsible action to help peers in distress; they empower the helpers by enhancing their sense of social usefulness and self-esteem. There is also some evidence that, over time, they improve the social climate of the school (Naylor and Cowie, forthcoming). Following the introduction of a peer support programme in one school, it became more acceptable for all pupils (not only the peer helpers) to report bullying incidents when they saw them; a sample of pupils who were interviewed about their perceptions of bullying in their school reported that the atmosphere in the school had changed and that it 'felt safer to tell' (Sharp et al., 1994).

Overall, research seems to show that the establishment of a peer support service can benefit the helped, the helpers and the school as a whole. As it would be expected, the children in need feel safer and more secure when there is a peer support system in place in their schools.

The findings for peer helpers are also consistent and clear (Cowie, in press, 1998). Peer support schemes improve self-confidence, give young people useful skills, enhance their responsibility and give them a useful opportunity to act pro-socially in their school. These enhanced personal qualities seemed to arise from a number of sources. First, there is involvement in teamwork as an integral part of planning, advertising and publicizing the service, implementing it, and talking about the experience in school assemblies and to external bodies. Interview responses give a clear indication of the value to these young people of addressing a real problem in their school community and being given the opportunity to tackle it. In some cases the publicity goes beyond the school to the outside community and attracts considerable media attention: 'It generally improves communication skills from speaking to small groups to up to a few hundred people . . . It is a challenge' (boy peer supporter, quoted in Cowie, in press, 1998). The young people appreciate public awareness of their action.

Second, peer supporters consistently comment favourably on the value of the communication skills they learn in the course of training. These skills include active, empathic listening, summarizing and reflecting back the accounts and narratives of peers in the role of 'clients', allowing space and time for the expression of emotions, learning not to offer advice too early, and collaborating with a peer to develop a problem-solving stance towards interpersonal issues. The value of this kind of experience cannot be underestimated since the skills can be transferred to other aspects of the young person's relationships with others.

Third, there are indications from secondary school peer helpers that the process of supervision is a beneficial one in terms of developing a vocabulary to capture the nuances of emotion, and in developing a reflective stance towards the interpersonal difficulties of both themselves and others. One benefit seems to be a growing awareness that other peer helpers experienced similar difficulties to themselves in dealing with others' distress.

In most studies, both peer helpers and teachers consistently report a general improvement in the ethos of the school: 'It creates a symbiotic ethos, feeling safer. People are looking out for one another. We're quite together as a school' (counsellor, secondary school, quoted in Cowie, in press, 1998).

Pupils in the school as a whole become more open to the idea that a problem may be profitably shared with another rather than keeping it to themselves. Where bullying was the focus, the peer helpers and teachers also report that pupils in general became more likely to view 'telling a teacher' about a bullying incident as a positive action rather than a betrayal of peer values. The benefits of peer support can be summarized as follows:

- children in need are given support and confidence
- a safer climate is created in schools
- bystanders are given a structure within which to offer help
- young people are offered training in valuable skills of helping, communication and empathy for others
- vulnerable children are helped to make friends
- there is an opportunity to practise citizenship in the real-life setting of the school
- the practice of peer support provides a preparation for the roles and responsibilities of adult life.

Difficulties arising

However, despite the benefits reported above, the implementation of peer support in schools is often hampered by ambivalent attitudes on the part of staff and students. Although there is strong evidence that this type of intervention is effective, there are widely expressed fears on the part of some adults that the young peer helpers are not up to the task. These teachers express anxiety that the pupils will lose motivation, that they lack appropriate training and even that they may do damage. Peer helpers typically perceived such statements as indicative of adult reluctance to share power:

> 'There was initial resistance from the staff. They were unwilling to give students the responsibility. The staff didn't really understand what we were doing, so we gave a small presentation in a staff meeting which helped to rectify this. But communication with staff has been a big problem.' (secondary school boy peer helper, quoted in Cowie, in press, 1998)

Although it was reported in this study that some of these teachers eventually became convinced of the peer helpers' skill over time, others remained sceptical.

Naylor and Cowie (forthcoming) carried out a survey in 65 schools with a peer support system in place; questionnaires were completed by actual or potential users of the system in Years 7 and 9, by peer supporters, by teachers who ran the system, and by teachers who had no direct involvement with the system. The survey revealed a dearth of men teachers and boy pupils in peer support systems; there was opposition to these systems from some teachers and from some male members of the peer group.

Peers can express hostility by undermining the peer helpers' belief in their own competence, or by deriding them as 'wimps', 'grasses', 'teachers' pets', or, as in one boys' school, 'queer supporters'. Boys seem to be especially vulnerable to this kind of criticism and it is notable that, in peer systems in mixed sex schools, girls typically outnumber boys at all stages of the process from application through selection, training and practice. Cowie (in press 1998), in a study of peer support services in nine schools, found that participation could open peer helpers to teasing or taunts from others. Male peer supporters in particular reported problems in integrating the prevailing 'macho' image of their peer group with a caring, helpful role. A minority of boy peer helpers seemed to be able to withstand this peer group pressure and acknowledge the benefits, but at every point – from recruitment through training and implementation – boys were under-represented and were most likely to drop out. The adults in charge of the peer support services were keenly aware of the need to involve boys as peer supporters but were unable to find a solution. If we reflect back on the findings of Salmivalli and her colleagues (Salmivalli et al., 1996), this is not surprising. The helpers, we suggest, are largely drawn from 'defenders' who, according to the research, are more likely to be girls.

There is also some evidence of peer group pressure *against* making use of a peer support service. For example MacLeod and Morris (1996), the authors of a survey sponsored by ChildLine, asked children about the policies which were in place in their schools to counteract bullying. These authors noted the 'star-tlingly little use' made of peer-led interventions, including 'bully lines, bully boxes, peer counselling, mentoring or mediation schemes' (p. 85). Yet the children in their sample talked frequently about the value to them of having someone to talk to about their troubles.

Charlton and David (1997) express surprise that so few schools make use of peers to offer personal and educational support to others and link this reluctance to an unwillingness to share power and give opportunities for responsible action in real-life settings:

> As ample evidence is now at hand showing clearly that this 'peer' resource can make valuable contributions to schools' efforts to improve their children's all-round performance, it is surprising that so few schools make use of it. Furthermore, this neglect becomes more be-wildering given a growing recognition of children's right to be listened to. (Charlton and David, 1997, p. 22)

A recurring issue noted by Cowie (in press, 1998) concerns the low allocation of time and resources to underpin the efforts of the adults and young people involved in peer support services. Very little time was allowed for the teachers to manage the services and to organize the necessary supervision. Consequently, this was usually done voluntarily during lunchtimes or after school. The question of the cost of training arose frequently, as did the issue of the supplying of private space for individual work with the young people who sought help. Naylor and Cowie (forthcoming) also expressed concern that insufficient attention was paid by schools in their survey to the key role of supervision in supporting the work and the personal well-being of the peer supporters them-selves. Although in all the schools in their study the headteachers expressed their commitment to the establishment of the peer support schemes, it could be argued that they had underestimated the extent of the financial and resource requirements needed for such a service to be maintained over time.

In general, studies of peer support indicate that there is a great deal of teacher and pupil enthusiasm for these schemes, not only as a way of challenging bullying but as a way, in the long term, of changing the ethos of a school to one of care. But a number of key points need to be taken into consideration if this approach is to be used to its full potential (Naylor and Cowie, forthcoming):

- All schools need to develop their strategies for systematically monitoring and evaluating the effectiveness of their peer support systems.
- Mixed sex schools need to continue to find ways of involving more men teachers and boy pupils in their peer support systems.
- All schools need to work at eliminating the opposition of some teachers to peer support systems.
- All schools need to ensure that peer supporters are provided with frequent and regular opportunities for being debriefed/supervised about their work.
- Peer supporters need ongoing support from the school as a whole if they are to be successful in their own supporting roles.

In conclusion, we would encourage all schools to consider initiating peer-led interventions as an important way of challenging the antisocial behaviour of some children.

6

DEALING WITH FEAR AND PHOBIAS

Understanding fear and phobia

Fear is a common feature of childhood; it is a normal reaction to a perceived threat. Ollendick et al. (1985) studied 126 children and young people aged between 7 and 18 and found the average number of their fears to be thirteen. The 'top ten' fears included:

- being hit by a car or truck
- not being able to breathe
- getting burned
- death/dead people
- bombing attacks/getting invaded
- getting poor grades
- a burglar breaking into the house
- parents arguing
- looking foolish
- falling from a high place/being sent to the principal.

The types of fears experienced by children and young people typically change with age. At around 12 months there is an increase in fear of strangers, strange objects and heights; from 12 to 24 months, children often experience fear of the toilet. From 2 to 4 years, fears of being alone, darkness, dogs and snakes begin to develop. Fears prompted by stories and TV characters – ghosts, burglars and kidnappers – begin to develop from 4 to 6 years. From 7 years onwards fears of injury, death and school become more predominant.

A phobia is a more extreme and persistent fear. It has been defined (by King et al. 1994) as a fear which:

- causes extreme anxiety

- is out of proportion to the demands of the situation
- cannot be explained or reasoned away
- is beyond voluntary control
- leads to avoidance of the feared situation
- persists over an extended period of time
- is unadaptive
- is not age or stage specific.

A feature of phobias is that they usually lead to the avoidance of the feared situation or object. The most common childhood phobias relate to the dark, water, animals and school. It is thought that there may be a biological mechanism which underlies phobias as they usually arise in relation to objects and situations which could present a threat to survival and are rarely caused by non-threatening objects (Seligman and Hager, 1972). It is sensible, in terms of survival, for children to fear certain things and, therefore, avoid them; when a child develops a phobia, it can be seen as this sensible fear 'going too far'.

Behaviourist learning theory has been used to explain how most phobias develop. Conditioning, modelling, instruction and positive reinforcement have all been identified as playing a part in the development of phobias. Evidence of conditioning arises through the prevalence of single or repeated traumatic events acting as a trigger for the phobia. Perhaps the most cited experimental evidence for conditioning is the famous 'Albert' experiment carried out by Watson and Raynor in 1920. Nine-month-old Albert showed no fear of live animals prior to the experiment. He did show fear when a loud clanging noise was made behind him. Watson and Raynor then made the loud noise whenever Albert touched the rat. After only seven such occasions, Albert began to cry when presented with the rat without the noise. For some children, phobias may develop through traumatic experiences. More frequently it seems that phobias are developed through modelling and reinforcement: the child observes a significant other displaying fear and anxiety and/or are reinforced for displaying fear or anxiety by parental reactions of reassurance, anger or affection. King et al. (1994) suggest that phobias may develop through any of these routes, but the final determinant is the child's own perceptions of self-efficacy and coping.

Childhood phobias are estimated to arise in about 3–8 per cent of the population and, without intervention, are usually 'outgrown' within five years (Agras et al., 1972). The one exception to this may be animal phobias, which often start before the age of 5 years and can last into adult life (Marks and Gelder, 1966).

Given the resistance of phobias to change, it may be reassuring that most will be outgrown. However, five years represents a significant proportion of a child's life and consequently inter-vention is important and worthwhile. Later in this chapter we will consider possible approaches to working with children and young people who have developed a phobia. First we will consider anxieties relating to school attendance in more detail.

Anxieties and fears about school are commonplace although King et al. (1994) suggest that just under 1 per cent of children and young people experience extreme anxiety relating to school at-tendance. Children and young people refuse to go to school for many different reasons. Whether the child is actually phobic about school or whether they are refusing to go, the impact on the child, on his or her educational progress and on the family can be quite severe and distressing. In the UK, legislation adds to the pressure on families because parents can be fined if their child repeatedly misses school.

School refusal often arises through a strong desire to stay at home or to avoid school. It is often preceded by change of school or home circumstances, illness or school-related upset. Staying at home may be intrinsically motivating: there may be fewer de-mands and challenges, and the youngster may be nurtured and cared for by parents in a way which does not happen in school. Some youngsters who have developed friendships within the community – perhaps with older people – may prefer to spend time with them than with peers in school. Some children and young people are very anxious about leaving their parents – they become concerned that something awful will happen to their parents while they are not there. This is often the case when a parent or relative has been injured or seriously ill. In these situations the youngster may have taken on the caring or parent-ing role and it can be hard for him or her to resume the role of child which is required in school. One student who was caring for her dying mother and having to take responsibility for her younger siblings, said:

'Before I come to school I've made breakfast and got them out to school . . . they're all shouting and screaming . . . set up my mum for the day and I get here and the maths teacher gives me a hard time for not having a calculator and I just think, "f*** off – what do you know about my life? What's a bloody calculator matter?" . . . and then I just have to get out of here . . . run away . . . I can't bear it . . . if I stay I'm just thinking, "Will she be dead when I get home?" '

Similarly, during divorce, children can assume household responsibilities which bind them strongly to the home. Fear of leaving the home may link with fear that when they return their remaining parent will also have disappeared.

There are often specific triggers for anxiety which leads to school refusal. Fear of academic or social failure may discourage attendance. Bullying is cited by 5 per cent of students as a reason for truanting (Sharp, 1995). For some secondary school aged students, the level of noise and movement in and around school causes extreme stress. An upsetting incident, such as wetting oneself in class, can lead to a reluctance to return. For younger primary aged children toileting arrangements can provoke anxiety, in particular when the school restrict opportunities for going to the toilet to specified times such as playtime and breaks. After even a short period of absence, re-entry can be extremely difficult. New friendships will have been formed so that it will not be easy for the youngster to resume old relationships. Even if the student has continued with school work from home, the pace of the curriculum is fast and she or he will inevitably find it is difficult to keep up at first or that essential pieces of information are missing. When planning re-entry to school, consideration has to be given to both the social and the academic challenges the youngster will face. It will be necessary to discuss how students will be supported in each subject area so that they do not feel disadvantaged, as well as developing peer support networks to ease re-entry into the social milieu of the school.

Often, it is not only school or home factors which lead to school refusal but rather a mixture of both, as the following case study illustrates.

Case study

Jane was a 13-year-old student who attended a large secondary comprehensive school. There was a lot of bullying in her class, especially among the girls. Jane was physically and emotionally more mature than her peers. She was tall and slightly overweight. All of the other girls in the class were small and slight. She was often teased about her appearance and felt self-conscious about her size.

Her grades were quite poor and she found much of the work difficult. Her parents ran their own business and at weekends Jane helped out in the office. She was extremely competent in this position – carrying out a wide range of clerical and administrative duties for the family firm, building good relationships with clients and being able to converse confidently with a wide range of people. Jane underwent a minor operation and was away from school for two weeks. While she was recovering she helped out in the office with her parents. On her return to school, the bullying in class was particularly severe and Jane began to stay off school with various aches and pains. This went on for some months, with Jane's attendance becoming worse and worse until she was not going at all. Jane had begun to get extremely anxious about the idea of returning to school and would become distressed if her parents broached the subject. Jane's motivation to stay at home where she was safe, cared for and felt extremely competent was far greater than her desire to go to school where she felt she did not fit in, was excluded and bullied. Her academic motivation was low because she knew she could enter the family business without qualifications.

Ways of working with fears and phobias

Systematic desensitization
Systematic desensitization was developed by Wolpe in 1958 and is a commonly used approach to children and young people who experience phobias. Systematic desensitization is based on teaching the individual how to consciously relax themselves and then gradually increase exposure to the cause of the phobia. During the relaxation training the individual is encouraged to tense and then relax each muscle group within the body. Two or three muscle groups are focused on in each fifteen to twenty minute session, usually starting with the dominant hand and arm. Once the child has been taught to relax the different muscle groups separately, he or she can learn how to relax the whole body simultaneously. The next stage is to develop a hierarchy of anxiety. Here, the individual is asked to rate between fifteen and twenty-five different situations which relate to the phobia on a scale of 0 to 100: 0 is comfortable and relaxed; 100 is extremely anxious. The situations can then be ranked in order of level of anxiety. For young children, the parents or carers may have to provide this information. The following is an anxiety hierarchy for Jane:

1   reading a story about school
2   watching a programme on TV about school
3   hearing my friends talking about what they did at school today
4   Dad saying, 'It's school tomorrow, go and get your bag ready.'
5   waking up in the morning and seeing my uniform hanging on the door
6   eating breakfast in my school uniform
7   picking up my bag
8   going out of the front door
9   waiting at the bus stop with all the other kids
10 going into the school library
11 walking across the school yard
12 walking through the corridors full of children with people noticing me
13 getting near to the form room
14 seeing the form room door
15 walking through the form room door
16 looking round the room to find somewhere to sit
17 my friend saying, 'Oh you're back at school.'

The hierarchy is then used in conjunction with relaxation to 'desensitize'. Again using Jane's case as an example: Jane relaxes and, once relaxed, the therapist describes one of the situations on the hierarchy, starting with the least anxiety provoking. Jane imagines herself within the scenario and indicates how anxious she feels. Once she is able to imagine herself in the scene without feeling anxious, she progresses to the next situation on the hierarchy and so on. This process can be used with real life situations as well as imagery, in fact with children and young people real life exposure can be more effective. With Jane, we used a combination of working imaginatively within her own home and progressing to visits to the school. Eventually Jane was able to return to school and resume her classes.

Emotive imagery

This approach, developed by Lazarus and Abramovitz (1962), uses narrative to develop images which promote positive anxiety-reducing emotions such as competency, pride, and self-assertion. The positive images are used within a narrative which is similar to the child's own life. References to anxiety-provoking stimuli are gradually introduced into the narrative and the level of anxiety caused monitored. Positive images are developed through an exploration of the child's favourite hero/heroine or aspirations

and the storyline is constructed around this. Lazarus and Abramovitz describe a boy who was terrified of dogs. His fantasy was that
he would own and drive an Alfa Romeo sports car. The narrative
developed to work with this boy involved a detailed and elaborate story of him owning an Alfa Romeo and driving in it. Once
this image was well developed, the therapist made reference to a
dog sitting by a tree. Using this technique, the therapist gradually
introduced situations which would have provoked greater and
greater anxiety in other circumstances. The positive image of the
boy driving the Alfa Romeo seemed to enable him to control his
fear of dogs. Within three sessions there was a marked improvement in his phobia and within 12 months it had gone com-
pletely.

In Chapter 4, we considered the use of metaphor and narrative
as a helpful approach to exploring difficulties and developing
solutions. The relaxed state which children enter through emotive
imagery is very similar to the trance-like state described by
Benson (1995) induced by storytelling.

Flooding
Flooding involves exposing the child or young person to the most
anxiety provoking situation and maintaining the exposure until
the anxiety-reaction subsides. In the case of Jane, for example, the
young girl who was afraid of school, this would mean taking her
directly to the form room – the situation she felt most anxious
about – regardless of distress or resistance and keeping her there
until she calmed. Flooding is rarely used with children and young
people because of ethical concerns and because it is extremely
difficult to achieve. A truly phobic child will put up an immense
struggle if forced to confront the source of their anxiety. This
makes it not only physically hard to sustain but also extremely
distressing for the child and the adults involved.

Contingency management
The key elements of contingency management are reinforcement
of behaviours which are desirable to increase and reduction of
behaviours which are not. Contingency management is often used
to change behaviour generally. The behaviourist theory under-
pinning contingency management assumes that behaviours are
increased or sustained through reward. Behaviours which are not
rewarded will be reduced. The child is rewarded – by praise,
attention or tokens – when she or he increases contact with the

problematic situation or object. Careful analysis of the consequences of the phobia identifies possible rewards for the anxious
behaviour and these are reduced. For example, a child who is
afraid of dogs may be picked up and cuddled every time a dog is
near; this rewards the fearful behaviour. Any reactions which may
be seen as rewarding are stopped. When working with children
and young people who are afraid of school, a common feature of
the intervention programme is to make sure that being at home is
less rewarding than being at school. This will require the parents
or carers to introduce a structure for the day which includes
school work and excludes leisure activities such as watching
television, playing games, and shopping; other exclusions may
also be applied depending on the individual child.

Cognitive approaches
Cognitive approaches build upon the interactions between feeling,
thought and behaviour by using changes in thinking to influence
behaviour and emotion. Ellis (1970) proposed that most anxieties
and difficulties arise through irrational thinking – holding beliefs
and assumptions which are not logical or possible. Irrational
beliefs and assumptions are often characterized by emphatic self-
statements: 'I must always be polite', 'I must never be late'; or by
catastrophizing consequences: 'My parents will hate me if I'm
rude, and then it will be the end of the world.' Working with
youngsters who have phobias using a rational-emotional approach involves identifying what event or situation led to the
current situation and the self-talk which arose from this. Through
this self-talk it is usually possible to identify irrational beliefs.
Logical self-statements are devised to replace the irrational ones
and to support more logical and reasonable beliefs. For example, a
child who is afraid of dogs may believe: 'If a dog bites me I will
die.' More rational beliefs would be: 'If a dog bites me it will be
painful' and 'Most dogs will only bite if provoked.'

7

REJECTION AND VICTIMIZATION

Social acceptance is very important for children and young people. Close friendships and casual relationships provide youngsters with a network of support within which they can establish themselves as individuals and their identity as part of a social community. Silverman et al. (1995) interviewed 141 boys and 132 girls who were aged between 7 and 12 years and who attended school in Florida. They concluded that: 'Classmates provide children with a sense of acceptance and belonging, whereas close friendships provide intimacy, loyalty and emotional support' (p. 682).

From as young as 3 years of age children begin to form friendships with children outside their family group. They also begin to feel the pain and distress of social isolation – neglect, rejection and victimization (Rubin, 1982). Loneliness and relationship breakdown may be short term, with the child moving quickly on to develop new and different friendships. The array of feelings that relationship breakdown leads to includes depression, irritability, anger, resentment and self-blame. In turn this can affect self-esteem and feelings of competence. In the long term, persistent peer relationship difficulties have been linked with difficulties with later adjustment (see Erwin, 1993, for a review). In this chapter we will focus on an antisocial behaviour which is widespread in schools and which inevitably leaves children and young people feeling rejected and victimized: bullying.

Definition of bullying

In academic research, bullying behaviour has been ascribed three key defining features:

- it is a type of aggressive behaviour

- it involves a systematic abuse of power
- it occurs over a prolonged period of time.

The nature of the bullying behaviours can vary and can be physical, verbal or psychological. These behaviours may be overt or covert. They can be categorized along two dimensions: direct/ indirect and verbal/non-verbal (see Table 7.1).

Table 7.1 *Categorization of bullying behaviour using verbal/non verbal and direct/indirect as groupings*

	Verbal	Non-verbal
Direct	name calling, teasing, extortion	physical assault, damage to belongings
Indirect	sending nasty notes, graffiti	social exclusion

Bullying behaviour can occur between two people although it often takes place within larger groups. Indeed definitions arising from some Scandinavian researchers (Lagerspetz et al., 1982; Pikas, 1989) include group activity as a fourth key defining feature. Other features which are often referred to in relation to bullying behaviour include that it involves:

- intention to hurt (Tattum and Lane, 1989; Smith and Thompson, 1991)
- unprovoked behaviour (Rigby, 1996)
- helplessness of victim (Roland, 1989; Smith and Thompson, 1991).

The definition used by Dan Olweus (1991), and added to by Ahmad et al. (1991), describes bullying as:

> when another child or group of children say nasty or unpleasant things to him or her. It is also bullying when a child is hit, kicked, threatened, locked inside a room, sent nasty notes, or when no-one ever talks to them and things like that. These things can happen frequently and it is difficult for the child being bullied to defend himself or herself. It is also bullying when a child is teased repeatedly in a nasty way. It is not bullying when two children of about the same strength have the odd fight or quarrel.

Prevalence of bullying behaviour in schools

There have been several large-scale international studies of bullying in schools. Most have used a self report questionnaire which asks subjects to reflect on the last term and report the extent to which they have been bullied or bullied others (for example, Olweus, 1978, 1991; O'Moore and Hillery, 1989; Mellor, 1990; Whitney and Smith, 1993). Whitney and Smith (1993) in their extensive survey of 6758 primary and secondary school-aged students discounted reports of infrequent bullying. The students had to report being bullied more than once or twice during the term to be included. On the basis of these more stringent criteria, Whitney and Smith found that about 27 per cent of primary aged students and 10 per cent of secondary aged students had been bullied during that term; 10 per cent of primary and 4 per cent of secondary students reported being bullied more than once a week through the term. Other studies which use the same definition have found similar levels of bullying (Rigby and Slee, 1991; Mooij, 1993; Pepler et al., 1993). When less persistent bullying is included higher levels are suggested – between 40 and 60 per cent of students reporting being bullied 'once in a while' or 'this term' (Branwhite, 1994; O'Moore and Hillery, 1989; Pepler et al., 1993; Rigby and Slee, 1991). Smith and Levan (1995) asked 60 6- and 7-year-olds whether they had been bullied that day, that week and that term (there were no references to the extent of bullying experienced): 10 per cent of the children reported being bullied that day; 23 per cent had been bullied that week; and 43 per cent had been bullied that term. Evidence also suggests that between 4 and 5 per cent of students are bullied for more than one year (La Fontaine, 1991; Thompson, 1995; Rigby, 1996). The studies also note that there are large variations in levels of reported bullying between some schools, and some classes and year groups within the schools.

Collectively, these studies suggest that around 1 in 2 students experience occasional bullying during any school term; 1 in 4 in primary school and 1 in 10 in secondary school are bullied more often – at least more than once or twice in any term; and 1 in 10 primary aged students and 1 in 25 secondary aged students are persistently and frequently bullied – possibly every day. Bullying is a fairly common experience for children and young people. All schools probably have some bullying.

Most common forms of bullying behaviour

It is hardly surprising that when asked to define bullying young children refer to being hit and kicked or being called nasty names. These are the most prevalent forms of bullying. Whitney and

Smith (1993) found that 50 per cent of primary-aged students and 62 per cent of secondary-aged students who reported being bullied had been called names; 36 per cent and 26 per cent respectively had been physically hurt.

Age, gender and victimization

Age and gender differences in types of bullying behaviour have been recorded. Whitney and Smith (1993) found that boys were more likely to be physically hit and threatened. Girls were more likely to experience verbal and indirect bullying. These gender differences were apparent across both the primary and secondary phases. Björkqvist et al. (1992) found that younger children and boys engaged mostly in direct physical bullying; older children and girls used social exclusion more often. They concluded this was related to developmental phases, and suggested that with maturity bullying behaviour becomes more subtle and, therefore, more indirect because individuals are reluctant to attract peer or adult disapproval. Their research into adult covert aggression supports this theory (Björkqvist et al., 1994). Anne Campbell (1993) argues that boys and girls are equally aggressive. From an early age boys are taught to use aggression instrumentally to achieve their goals – through rough and tumble play, 'tackling' to get a football, etc.; girls, however, are taught to suppress and control their aggression and, therefore, are much more likely to use indirect and covert aggression to manage their relationships. Possibly, boys have clearer rules about aggression – they know how to limit the force they use to achieve their goals whereas girls, because they are discouraged from using overt aggression, do not have 'boundaries' and therefore tend to either disguise what they are doing or go 'out of control'.

The social context of bullying

The social context of bullying can be considered in terms of the context of the school and the context of the peer group. The variations in levels of bullying found between schools and classes within schools by both Whitney and Smith (1993) and Olweus (1991) suggest that social context contributes to the likelihood of bullying taking place. Whitney and Smith found that schools which scored highly on a scale of social disadvantage were slightly but significantly more likely to experience higher levels of bullying, as did schools where more pupils reported not having anyone to play with. Ethnic mix of the school population and size of school or class did not relate to variations in levels of reported bullying. Ziegler and Rosenstein-Manner (1991), in a study of Toronto schools, found higher levels of bullying in inner city schools. In a comparison of adult recollections of being bullied in both single and mixed sex schools, Dale (1991) found that there were higher levels of reported bullying in single sex than co-educational schools. Stephenson and Smith (1991) investigated bullying in 26 primary schools in Cleveland. They looked closely at the 6 schools with the highest levels of bullying and the 6 schools with the lowest levels of bullying. They found in the schools with lower levels of bullying, the Headteacher: 'tended to express articulate, considered views on bullying and attached importance to controlling and preventing its occurrence' (p. 136). Research into locations in which bullying takes place also supports the notion that the environment influences levels of bullying. Most bullying occurs in the playground (Mellor, 1990; Whitney and Smith, 1993) when supervision is minimal and there is a more informal atmosphere.

Perhaps the most convincing evidence for the impact of the school as an organization on levels of bullying arises from intervention studies. Roland (1993) identifies that levels of bullying fall in schools which systematically tackle the problem. Olweus (1991) found that schools which developed and implemented strategies against bullying experienced significant reductions – on average cuts of 50 per cent. A similar reduction was found in primary schools which had invested considerable effort in establishing anti-bullying policies in the DFE funded Sheffield anti-bullying project (Smith and Sharp, 1994). Where schools had done little to address the problem, levels of bullying had increased or stayed the same. The key ingredient for success in all these projects seemed to be the involvement of the wider school community, including the students themselves, in the agreement of a set of guidelines for behaviour. In the process of achieving these guidelines, there was extensive discussion of what bullying is, and an emphasis on collective responsibility in both preventing it and responding to it. The high profile of the anti-bullying policy established bullying as an unacceptable behaviour. The intervention extended beyond the few individuals who were directly involved and established bullying as a complex, social phenomenon which required wide-ranging action.

These intervention programmes have stressed in particular the importance of involving and empowering the peer group in reducing bullying (Sharp and Cowie, 1994; Sharp and Thompson, 1994). Teacher estimations of bullying behaviour are notoriously poor. In contrast, the accuracy of peer nominations in relation to bullying behaviour suggests that the peer group know only too well who is doing what to whom. Furthermore, studies of social networks suggest that the peer group is a powerful influence on levels of aggression. De Rosier et al. (1994) studied the behaviour of 125 7- and 9-year-old boys in 22 experimental play groups. They observed and noted behaviour before, during and after aggressive incidents as well as during cooperative periods. They found aggressive behaviour increased during active, rough and tumble play and teasing. They also found that when the by-standers to an aggressive bout all sided with the victim of the incident, this resulted in an increase in rough and tumble and put-downs. Wachtel (1973) suggested that highly aggressive children deliberately set up aggressive incidents so that they can be observed by peers.

Adler and Adler (1995) investigated the dynamics of pre-adolescent cliques over a period of seven years. Their study provides a fascinating insight into the power relations of young people and how bullying behaviour is often a function of peer group formation and maintenance. The reader is left with an all too clear impression of the nastiness and brutality of these groups. Adler and Adler define cliques as:

> circles of power wherein leaders attain and wield influence over their followers by cyclically building them up and cutting them down, first drawing them into the elite inner circle and allowing them to bask in the glow of popularity and acceptance, and then reducing them to positions of dependence and subjugation by turning the group against them. (1995, p. 145)

The leader of the clique and the other members use bullying tactics to maintain or boost their own position within the group and to control the behaviour and attitudes of others. The strategies used by the cliques included:

- recruitment techniques which promote the exclusivity and, therefore, the desirability of the clique
- deliberate wooing of individuals so that they abandoned their usual friendship groups, became isolated and, therefore, more dependent on the clique

- setting one person against another by using overt ridicule and derision
- picking on low status people outside the group
- alternate wooing and derision of people within the group
- urging others to pick on or ridicule others
- stigmatizing a particular individual and rejecting them
- expelling someone from the clique.

They quote Craig, a 'clique follower':

> 'Basically the people who are the most popular, their life outside in the playground is picking on people who aren't as popular, but are in the group. But the people just want to be more popular so they stay in the group. They just kind of stick with it, get made fun of, take it . . . They come back every day, you do more ridicule, more ridicule, more ridicule, and they just keep taking it because they want to be more popular and they actually like you but you don't like them. That goes on a lot, that's the main thing in the group. You make fun of someone, you get more popular, because insults is what they like. They like insults.' (Adler and Adler, 1995, p. 154)

The influence of the clique extends beyond the immediate peer group and has a significant effect on relationships throughout that year group. In the UK, these cliques would most certainly match with the descriptions of bullying gangs found in classes which report high levels of bullying. However, the fact that levels of bullying can be reduced (Smith and Sharp, 1994) indicates that the destructive behaviour of Adler and Adler's 'cliques' does not have to be the norm.

Finally, these studies remind us that an interactionist approach to understanding bullying is important. The bullying relationship is a social relationship and it is influenced by the social dynamics of the immediate peer group, the wider peer group, the systems and procedures within the school, and the ethics and mores of the community.

Consequences of being bullied

Most of the research on bullying to date has focused on the nature and extent of the behaviour rather than the consequences for either the victim or the bully. It is unfortunate that the questionnaire designed by Olweus and since used so widely only includes one question about the impact of bullying on individuals, and that is asked of witnesses. Olweus (1980) found that students who were persistently bullied were more anxious and insecure than other students, had a negative view of themselves, were often lonely and neglected by peers, and generally had low self-esteem. Rigby and Slee (1991) reported that bullied students showed slightly lower self-esteem than non-bullied peers but also noted that gender was more associated with variations in self-esteem than victimization. A further study (Rigby and Slee, 1991) found that students who were being bullied 'at least once a week' scored significantly more highly than non-bullied students on a general health questionnaire. The bullied students reported higher levels of somatic complaints, general depression and suicidal thoughts. Haselager and Van Lieshout (1992) found that bullied students are more likely to show signs of depressive distress, negative self-evaluations and physical complaints than other classmates. They were also more likely to be rejected by peers, less likely to be chosen as a best friend, and shy and withdrawn.

Neary and Joseph (1994) investigated self-worth, depression and victimization in 60 11- and 12-year-old girls. They found that the girls who had scored more highly on a victimization scale also reported lower global self-worth, and poorer self-perceptions in relation to academic competence, social relationships, attractiveness and conduct. Branwhite (1994) in a questionnaire survey of 836 11- and 12-year-olds asked what situations the students found most stressful. Being called names ranked fourth most stressful, below loss of a pet, loss of a relative and going to hospital. Hoover et al. (1992) found that of their sample of 207 12- and 18-year-olds, three-quarters had been bullied at some time in their school career and 14 per cent felt that this had been a 'very severe problem' for them. Boulton and Underwood (1992) interviewed 122 8- and 10-year-olds; 80 per cent of those who had experienced bullying reported feeling better about themselves prior to the onset of bullying.

Reid (1989) investigated reasons for truancy and found that 15 per cent of persistent absentees said they had stayed away from school initially because of being bullied; 19 per cent continued to stay away from school because of this. Balding et al. (1996) carried out a questionnaire survey of 11,000 11- to 16-year-olds from 65 schools. Some of the questions in the survey related to fear of going to school, fear of being bullied and self-esteem. They found that of 4989 Year 8 students, 21.3 per cent of boys and 28.2 per cent of girls, reported that they were sometimes afraid to go to school because of bullying. For 2.4 per cent of boys and 3.1 per cent of girls, this was a feeling they had 'very often'. These students reported higher frequencies of illness and disease and generally presented as more anxious. They found that students who did not fear bullying were more satisfied with life, had higher self-esteem, had greater feelings of personal control, felt fit, felt confident with the opposite sex and were taller. In this study we have no information about actual experiences of being bullied and so, therefore, it is difficult to know whether their higher levels of anxiety generally also led to a fear of being bullied or their fear of bullying actually arose from being bullied. Pervin and Turner (1994) surveyed 147 13- and 14-year-old students in one secondary school; 77 per cent of the boys and 89 per cent of the girls who had experienced bullying found it either worrying or frightening. Two students had changed schools because of the bullying. Sharp (1995) found that up to one-third of bullied students reported impaired concentration, psychosomatic illness, disturbed sleep. Some students would truant to avoid being bullied and as many as 13 per cent reported hurting themselves. Recent work carried out in Australia (Rigby, 1997) has linked repeated bullying with suicide attempts in adolescents.

Gay, lesbian and bisexual youth

In a recent survey of the long-term consequences of victimization at school, Rivers (1997a) found that, of the 190 gay, lesbian and bisexual adults in his survey, 53 per cent recalled having contemplated self-harm or suicide because they were being bullied. Furthermore, 40 per cent said that they had attempted to hurt themselves or take their own lives at least once, with three-quarters of those (30 per cent of the total sample) indicating that they had tried on more than one occasion. In a comparative study conducted in the USA, of 194 gay, lesbian and bisexual young adults (aged 15–21 years) surveyed from 14 community youth groups, Hershberger and D'Augelli (1995) found that 42 per cent of their sample had attempted to take their own lives because of the hostility they had faced both in school and in the wider community. Recent reports have suggested that in addition to truancy and academic failure, characteristics of low self-esteem, depression and anxiety are also common (Hunter and Schaecher, 1987).

Rivers (1997b) has argued that the safety of all young people is a non-negotiable maxim of education which should never be compromised because of an individual's cultural background, religious beliefs, gender or sexual orientation. Yet, all too often, it seems that where a young person has been bullied because of his or her actual or perceived sexual orientation, schools have failed to take action and allowed the cycle of violence to continue. Research suggests that the potential effects of not providing a safe environment for the education of young gay men, lesbians and bisexual men and women carry on into adulthood. Here one young gay man recalls his experience:

> 'The only method I found to block out what was going on around me was to create a mental wall and solely concentrate on school work. The over-riding commitment to my work was shown by my studying each and every night immediately I got in, finishing around ten o'clock with a break for tea. My social life was practically zero for five years. This reliance on academic achievement to bolster self-worth, coupled with an innate desire to strive for excellence, created more and more pressure until my final year at university when a series of anxiety attacks resulted in my not taking my exams.
>
> In many ways I became a recluse, not venturing out on my own except when I had to attend school. I refused to take my dog for a walk because I feared running into "lads" who would start with the verbal abuse. I still experience this fear when I go out and when passing groups of lads. In some ways I was lucky that the mental abuse did not run to violence. However, the mental pain I went through was significant and only after seeing a counsellor last year was I able to unlock that particular door. I have already described how my behaviour is still affected by my experience and I believe what happened at school also helped delay my "coming out" both to myself and my parents/ friends.' (Rivers, 1997b, pp. 41–42)

As the above excerpt demonstrates, coming out became that much more difficult for those young lesbians, gay men and bisexual men and women who were bullied/harassed at school. In addition, as the following account illustrates, feelings of helplessness, isolation and low self-worth can continue for many years and, if left unchecked, can result in desperate and uncalculated acts of self-harm:

> 'I think by the time I'd got to nineteen, twenty or twenty-one, I realised that if I was going to have any future, I was going to have to tell someone I was gay and it all hung on that . . . everything hung on that . . . The whole "coming out" process took years. I did it bit by bit by bit, but I had to go really low, sink to a very very low low point when I was about – a bit older than I said – twenty-two when I did overdose on sleeping tablets accidentally. It wasn't an attempt to die, but I did overdose and that would be the lowest you would get – the absolute rock bottom – there was seriously something wrong. I knew what was wrong, it was just that I wasn't being honest with myself. But, once I made the leap or whatever, that changed by telling somebody then

things very, very slowly and very, very gradually began to get better bit by bit by bit.' (Rivers, 1997b, pp. 41–2)

Lesbian, gay and bisexual youth are no different from any other group of young people, they too require support from teachers and the education system in general to help them develop a positive self-image and achieve academically. As Rivers (1997b) says, 'we should focus upon the action society needs to take to safeguard the rights of young gay men and lesbians rather than expecting so many of them to give up their youth' (p. 45).

Bullying can have serious psychological, educational and emotional consequences. It is important that adults who work with bullied students take action against it.

Taking action against bullying

Intervention studies have demonstrated that the most effective interventions against bullying are those which:

- involve the whole school community
- lead to a clear understanding of what bullying is and what to do about it
- result in consistent prevention and response.

Many schools achieve this kind of systematic and consistent approach by developing a whole school policy. The policy describes what bullying is and what should be done about it. Most importantly, it is achieved through a process of discussion between staff, students and parents. It is probably the act of going through this process which begins to bring about change, whereas actually putting the policy into practice maintains and institutionalizes it. This is because bullying is a widespread, persistent behaviour and these types of behaviour are usually embedded within the organization (Pearlin, 1991). They are, therefore, very resistant to individual solutions, requiring change at the group or organizational level instead. The extensive discussion of bullying, why it matters and what should be done about it which takes place while developing a whole school policy, acts as a powerful lever to bring about institutional change.

The practice which results from the policy will include:

- curriculum teaching to increase social awareness, relationship management skills and conflict resolution
- behaviour management system which reinforces appropriate social behaviour

- opportunities for students to discuss problems in peer relationships and develop solutions to these problems
- definite guidelines for immediate, short-term and long-term action when bullying arises
- definite guidelines for action should bullying reoccur among the same students
- ways of supporting persistently bullied students.

Stopping the bullying

The most effective early interventions for stopping bullying seem to be problem solving approaches which involve the students directly involved meeting together to agree how they will behave differently. An example of a problem-solving group approach is the 'method of shared concern', developed by Swedish psychologist, Anatol Pikas (Pikas, 1989). This approach was evaluated during the Sheffield-based anti-bullying project and found to be successful in around 75 per cent of cases (Smith and Sharp, 1994). A similar approach is the 'no-blame approach' developed by Maines and Robinson (1997). Their evaluations suggest a similarly high success rate in stopping the bullying. The method of shared concern consists of individual discussions with each student who has been involved in the bullying. During these one-to-one 'chats' the adult begins by neutrally stating that bullying is happening and by asking the student to talk about what is going on. Most students will respond to this by briefly describing some of the bullying behaviour, even though they may not acknowledge their own involvement and are not likely to 'tell the whole story'. The adult can then suggest that the victim is 'having a bad time'. When the student agrees, the adult can legitimately ask the student to suggest ways in which she or he could help the bullied student. The adult also talks with the bullied student. In this discussion, the adult and student work together to identify action that the bullied student could take to avoid or to challenge the bullying behaviour. An example of how a one-to-one 'chat' might proceed is shown in Figure 7.1.

The initial meetings are followed up a week to ten days later. If there has been improvement in relationships, a group meeting is held. The purposes of the group meeting are to acknowledge within it that everybody has changed their behaviour and to identify long-term solutions – how can they maintain these changes? What will they do if someone starts the bullying again?

> *Teacher*:   (*Waits for student to glance at her.*) Jo, I hear that Sam is being bullied.
> *Jo*:   It's not me.
> *Teacher*:   (*Silence*)
> *Jo*:   Well, a few people are calling her names and stuff like that. It's not serious – she asks for it.
> *Teacher*:   So Sam is having a bad time in school.
> *Jo*:   I suppose so.
> *Teacher*:   What could you do to help Sam?
> *Jo*:   Me?
> *Teacher*:   Yes.
> *Jo*:   (*Long silence.*) I suppose I could tell the others not to call her names.
> *Teacher*:   That would be really helpful. Try that over the next week and we will meet next week to see how you have got on. OK – you can go back to your class now.
> *Jo*:   Is that it? OK. See you next week.

Figure 7.1   *An initial one-to-one 'chat' between a teacher and a student who has been bullying a peer using the 'method of shared concern'.*

Because bullying is a persistent behaviour, adults who are working with students who are in a bullying relationship will need to follow up reasonably regularly to check that the bullying has not resumed, either with the initial victim or someone else.

Involvement of parents may also be a powerful force for stopping the bullying reoccurring. As when working with the students, it will be important to adopt a problem-solving rather than a blaming approach. If parents feel blamed they will become defensive and resistant to even agreeing that their son or daughter may have bullied someone else. There are rarely neutral witnesses to bullying behaviour and very often there are two groups of students providing conflicting but convincing accounts of events. A starting point for work with students and parents can be the statement that this is a relationship which is not working well. This avoids entrenchment because people feel blamed but acknowledges that there is a problem which needs resolving. From such a starting point, the adult can facilitate the development of a solution which involves both students and their families and is, therefore, more likely to be enduring.

The responses we have discussed so far occur after the bullying relationship has been reported or identified by an adult worker. Another source of intervention is more immediate: the peer group. There are often bystanders who witness bullying behaviour. Too often, these classmates will ignore or collude with the bullying behaviour. They may giggle when someone is called a nasty name, ostracize the victim, or physically turn away when the bullying takes place. When working with the peer group to encourage collective responsibility for tackling bullying, we can teach students how to challenge bullying behaviour. This may include:

- verbally supporting the bullied student – for example, 'Leave him alone.', 'That's not fair', 'Just ignore them.'
- physically supporting the victim – for example, standing close to the bullied student, leading them away from the bullying situation
- seeking help from a teacher or other adult.

These peer interventions are low level but can make the difference between the bullying stopping in the early stages or continuing for weeks, months or even years.

Bullying behaviour must be challenged. It can be stopped by:

- involving the students and their families in problem-solving approaches
- peer intervention.

When tackling bullying, adults should remember that bullying is difficult to prove, easy to overlook and resistant to change.

Supporting the bullied student

Individual interventions which involve the bullied student 'standing up for themselves' are unlikely to be successful in their own right when a bullying relationship has already been established. Interventions which take over from the bullied student and do not allow them to respond themselves can increase feelings of helplessness. A balanced approach is more helpful – supporting the student in making an assertive response.

Teaching the student to be more assertive may not stop the bullying but it can:

- help the student to cope more effectively with the bullying
- help the student to stop bullying becoming established in the first place.

When bullying has become persistent, a combination of direct adult intervention, peer support and student assertiveness may be required to shift the relationship.

Bullied students can be taught to:

- be assertive
- seek help from peers or adults
- leave the bullying situation as quickly as possible.

Assertive behaviour involves being clear, direct and calm. It is based on mutual respect for self and others and helps to de-escalate a conflict situation. Assertive behaviour combines verbal statements with calm and confident body language. Bullied students are likely to need to rehearse and practise verbal and non-verbal assertive behaviour. As bullying is often repetitive, it is possible to re-enact the bullying situation and enable the student to try out appropriate assertive strategies.

There are a number of different types of assertive statement: *responsive*, where you try to find out the other person's viewpoint; *empathic*, where you acknowledge the other person's feelings; *discrepancy*, where you point out what was agreed and what is happening now; and so on. The most effective when confronting bullying are *basic* – a simple statement of what you do or do not want to happen, for example, 'I want you to stop calling me names', or *consequential* – pointing out the consequences of continuing with the behaviour, for example, 'If you continue to call me names, I shall report you to the Headteacher.' The student may need to repeat the basic statement two or three times, and must do so in a calm, clear and direct manner – regardless of how intimidating or threatening his or her tormentors are trying to be.

Staying calm in the face of aggression is easier said than done and students will probably need to be taught stress management techniques such as physical relaxation, breath control or visualization to help them to achieve this.

Assertiveness, conflict resolution and stress management are all helpful skills for bullied students to develop. By themselves, they may only help the student to cope more effectively with the bullying situation or to stop new bullying relationships from being established. In persistent relationships, these skills need to be combined with other interventions to stop the bullying.

8

DISRUPTIVE AND AGGRESSIVE BEHAVIOUR

Disruptive and aggressive behaviour rarely 'just happens'; it is usually linked to some current, past or previous experience. Effective intervention requires careful analysis of the behaviour itself and its causes. In summary, we have to ask ourselves: 'what is happening?' and 'why is it happening?' before we can answer the question: 'what can we do about it?' When tackling disruptive or aggressive behaviour it is more effective to identify ways of preventing it arising again than to focus solely on responding to it. In this chapter we will describe a framework for developing interventions for children and young people who are persistently disruptive and aggressive.

Disruption and aggression are behaviours which may be appropriate in some settings but usually hinder effective education. In 1989, a government-led inquiry into discipline in schools identified that major incidents of aggression were relatively rare in schools. What caused teachers most concern were 'petty disruptions' within lessons and around the school. One in three secondary school teachers reported being most disturbed by students talking out of turn, distracting other students, avoiding work, swearing, and verbally harassing other students. The inquiry went on to identify common features of schools which had low levels of disruptive and aggressive behaviour. These will be described later in this chapter.

Aggression is a term used to describe a wide range of behaviours, thoughts and feelings. Aggressive behaviours are those which could or do cause hurt, injury or death. Hurt could be physical or psychological. Sometimes, as adults who work with children and young people, we may label a behaviour as disruptive or aggressive when we actually mean that we do not like or approve of that behaviour. In other words, we find the behaviour challenging or disturbing. It may be that the behaviour is challenging to us because we have no strategies for responding to it – we therefore feel helpless or incompetent. Whenever we encounter challenging behaviour, one of our first questions needs to be: 'What is it about this behaviour that I find challenging?' Often, we become concerned about disruptive or aggressive behaviour when it is repeated or seems habitual. The re-occurrence of the behaviour may be interpreted as our ineffectiveness. This challenge to our competence can lead to inappropriate internal or external attributions such as 'I must be useless as a teacher/parent/worker' or 'What can you expect from a kid like that . . . she's just like her father/they're all like that in that family' and so on. Either attribution is likely to lead to less effective intervention and increased stress, which will in turn lead to more problematic behaviour. When tackling disruptive and aggressive behaviour, we need to recognize the role our own emotional response to the behaviour plays in our perceptions of the behaviour as problematic and our effectiveness in managing it. Any intervention should include strategies for enhancing our stress management and emotional coping.

There are a number of different psychological theories which can help us to understand why we behave as we do. Ethologists consider the biological determinants of behaviour. They have studied aggression extensively both in animals and in humans, and have identified a number of different kinds of aggression which they consider to be related to species survival. These include fear-induced aggression which is defensive; parental aggression which arises when a significant other is threatened; predatory aggression to meet basic needs; territorial aggression to protect space; dominance which is aimed at attaining status in the social hierarchy and to gain resources, including mates; and emotional aggression which occurs in response to frustration or attack by others (Weisfeld, 1994). Behavioural theorists believe that behaviour is learnt and shaped by reinforcement; our habitual behaviours are those which have been rewarded in some way. Behavioural theorists believe that behaviour can be changed by manipulating environmental contingencies. Cognitive psychologists emphasize perception and thought. This influences behaviour. Consequently by changing the way we think about things we can change the way we behave. Systemic psychologists consider behaviour to arise through the reciprocal interaction of individuals within groups and their environments. People who live or work together form a system and behave in ways which maintain homeostasis. This means that even if one person changes their behaviour, the rest of the people in the system will try to discourage them from changing or will change their behaviour to repair the 'imbalance' in the system. Systemic psychologists look not only at the individual but at the social dynamics of the group within which they are functioning. Behaviour change involves the whole system not just an individual within it.

All of these theories can be used to shape behaviour management and intervention programmes.

Prevention of disruptive and aggressive behaviour in schools

The Elton committee, which conducted the government inquiry into discipline in schools, found that schools whose students were well behaved shared some common features. The most important contributors were the attitudes and motivation of the Headteacher and staff (so that all staff looked forward to teaching and enjoyed being in the school and with the students) as well as a positive ethos which fostered a sense of community where everyone was overtly valued. The Elton Committee recommended that schools develop a whole school behaviour policy with clear principles, which is arrived at through wide consultation and the agreement of all staff. They suggested that it should:

- contain a minimum number of positively phrased guidelines for behaviour
- offer rewards for positive behaviour as well as sanctions for inappropriate behaviour
- avoid group punishments or punishments which involve humiliation
- be applied with consistency and fairness while still retaining a degree of flexibility for unusual circumstances
- provide direct action against bullying and harassment
- offer support for non-teaching as well as teaching staff
- be subject to regular evaluation and open to change
- address on-site and off-site behaviour.

Brighouse (1993) provides an example of a positively constructed whole school behaviour policy (1993, pp. 133–4):

SCHOOL CODE OF CONDUCT

This code has been produced after full consultation with students, staff, parents and governors.

INTRODUCTION

Students at XXXX have the right to an education which offers them the best opportunity to attain their potential.

Teachers are here to create the circumstances for this to happen; support staff, governors, parents and officers of the LEA to assist in the process. It is the right of every individual at XXXX to do these things without being hindered by others.

GUIDING PRINCIPLES

In order that the foregoing should happen, it is essential that everyone of us is:

CONSIDERATE:	respecting everyone else as an individual; making sure our words and actions do not cause inconvenience to anybody
COURTEOUS	being polite and helpful at all times
CO-OPERATIVE	being willing to work together
FRIENDLY	being on good terms with each other
HARD WORKING	doing our best
HONEST	being truthful
TRUSTING	accepting that others genuinely want help
RESPONSIBLE	being reliable and responsible for our actions; behaving as part of a community.

THE PRINCIPLES IN ACTION

What this means is that in practice we should all do the following:

BE PUNCTUAL:	avoid late arrival
SPEAK CONSIDERATELY:	avoid shouting, swearing and offensive language
BE READY FOR LESSONS:	have the necessary materials
CLEAR UP:	after lessons, break and dinner
MOVE IN AN ORDERLY WAY:	avoid running and use paths; hold doors open for other people
RESPECT THE ENVIRONMENT:	the grass, trees, hedges, buildings and furniture.

Whole school approaches influence behaviour in the school by developing a shared understanding and responsibility for action among all staff and students (Watkins, 1995). Such approaches emphasize that constructive behaviour management is everybody's responsibility, both in terms of self-management and in encouraging others to manage themselves. The development process brings together different groups within the school community, each of which examines their own contribution to effective behaviour management. The action taken by each group may be different but contributes to the shared goals of the school community, therefore achieving overall consistency in expectations of behaviour. This shaping of staff culture, relationships and boundaries impacts on the behaviour not only of individual students but of the wider student community (Miller, 1994).

The impact of the organizational and group context on behaviour is well documented (for example, Bull and Solity, 1989; Wheldall et al., 1981), and accordingly teachers need to work together to identify how they can manage the learning environment to increase constructive relationships and classroom order. The Elton Committee also noted that, at the classroom level, teachers needed to have a good knowledge of the subject they were teaching, know their students as individuals and have effective group management skills.

Docking (1993) identified five core management principles for the prevention and proactive management of student behaviour. These are:

- foreseeability: predicting the kinds of problems which might arise and developing explicit and constructive rules to guide behaviour and providing regular reminders of these;

- purposefulness: establishing a 'work-centred' environment within the classroom through careful planning and delivery of learning tasks, employing an assertive approach to teacher–student relationships, beginning and ending lessons in a calm and orderly manner, making sure that necessary materials are provided, matching the classroom environment to the task;

- accountability: helping students to develop feelings of commitment and responsibility through remaining vigilant, providing reminders and cues for on task behaviour, involving students in monitoring their own behaviour;

- constructiveness: enabling students to become successful learners through communicating positive expectations, encouraging students to recognize their own successes and to associate these with personal effort and practice, encouraging cooperation and encouraging

	parents to respond constructively to behaviour problems;
• collective responsibility:	actively involving students and staff in the establishment of classroom or whole school behaviour policy.

As we can see from Docking's five core principles, it is not only the development of guidelines for how to behave which is important; how the classroom is managed and organized, and how cooperative behaviour is encouraged, is also important. Thompson and Sharp (1995) criticize whole school approaches which focus on the regulation of discipline alone and fail to address relationship management, when many incidents of aggressive and disruptive behaviour arise through poorly managed conflict.

For conflict resolution to become a part of a school's behaviour management programme, staff themselves must be comfortable with conflict and feel confident to act as mediators in the first instance. Conflicts often arise when the actions of one person attempting to meet their needs appear to threaten, prevent, or hinder – or in some other way seem incompatible with – another person's efforts to meet their needs.

Creative conflict resolution involves clearly defining the problems that arise in conflict situations, and identifying and implementing solutions that are non-violent, that meet the needs of the people involved and, ideally, improve the relationships of those people. For staff and students to be able to engage in this process they need to be aware of what conflict and conflict resolution means, share their own experiences of this and gain insight into their own attitudes towards it. Additionally, they need to be willing to try out new approaches and, of course, they need to learn the skills which will enable them to do this.

Mediation and conflict resolution as an effective adult response to aggression between children and young people
Mediation and conflict resolution build upon listening skills by adding a step-by-step process which assists two or more people who are in conflict or who have experienced a breakdown of relationships to agree a mutually acceptable solution.

Key concepts There are three key concepts about conflict and disagreement which any person engaging in mediation or conflict resolution needs to understand.

1 **Conflict is not bad**. Staff and students may have mainly experienced negative attitudes about conflict: that it causes pain, fear and anger; spoils relationships; etc. These negative views are the results of messages about conflict such as 'Nice girls don't fight'; 'Don't get mad, get even', or 'If you can't say anything nice, don't say anything at all'. If individuals are to work constructively with conflict then they need to recognize that conflict is a normal and inevitable part of daily life. Furthermore, conflict can be positive. Through conflict we can learn more about ourselves and others, build better relationships, and learn new and better ways of sorting out problems.

2 **Conflict is not a contest**. If we assume that the outcome of a conflict will be for one person to 'win' and one person to 'lose', or at best for both people to give something up in order to reach a grudging compromise, then whatever the outcome at least one party will feel dissatisfied. Conflict should be viewed as a problem to be solved, so that all people get what they need. The key idea which underpins all creative conflict work is looking for a 'win–win' solution.

3 **Distinguish between what people want and why they want it**. In conflict situations, people often express their wishes (their position) rather than their needs or interests, although it is their unmet needs which underlie the conflict. For example, in the playground, two children are fighting over a bag. The adult asks them, 'What do you want?' They simultaneously reply, 'I want the bag.' The adult then asks each in turn, 'What do you need the bag for?' One child needs the bag itself to carry something in, the other needs something which is currently in the bag for their next lesson. Both can gain in this situation as long as they express their needs clearly.

The mediation/conflict resolution process In mediation, a neutral third person is called in to mediate. The mediator helps the children to find a solution but does not prescribe what they should do. She or he assists the individuals to recognize what they need and facilitates communication about this. Conflict resolution involves the same process but does not require a third party.

AN ENVIRONMENT FOR MEDIATION
The mediator will need to ensure that all people who have been involved in the conflict or dispute are present and that the room is

large enough for everyone to sit comfortably. The room should be private, with no interruptions. Seating arrangements should reflect the neutrality of the mediator.

INTRODUCTIONS

At the outset, the mediator should remind participants about the purpose of the mediation session, the steps that will be taken within mediation and repeat some ground rules about the mediation process. These are:

- mediation is voluntary
- the mediator remains neutral at all times
- whatever occurs within mediation should remain private and confidential
- the mediation session will last an agreed time
- all parties involved should listen to what is said without interrupting.

DEFINING THE PROBLEM

Each participant is given an agreed amount of time to describe their view of the problem situation, without interruptions. Feelings and concerns are heard as well as facts. The mediator clarifies the needs and interests of each party. At the end of each account the mediator summarizes what has been said to check for accuracy and to allow both parties to hear and reflect upon this.

IDENTIFYING KEY ISSUES

All issues arising from the accounts are listed on paper. They are divided into non-conflict issues and conflict related issues.

VISUALIZING AN IDEAL SOLUTION

Both parties state, ideally, what they would like to see happening in the future to improve the situation.

BRAINSTORM POSSIBLE OPTIONS

Both parties are encouraged to suggest solutions to any of the conflict issues identified earlier. These are written down.

MUTUAL EVALUATION OF POTENTIAL OUTCOMES OF OPTIONS

Until now, most communication has been directed at the mediator. Now the conversation will become more three-way. The mediator asks each party to think about the outcomes of each solution were it to be implemented, not only for themselves but for each other and for other people.

NEGOTIATION OF A PLAN OF ACTION AND AGREEMENT

The mediator asks the participants, 'Which of these solutions will most likely meet the needs of both of you?' One or two solutions are identified. These are clarified to ensure that each party knows who will do what, by when. These are then agreed. A written agreement of future actions is made and signed by all present. Both parties shake hands.

FOLLOW UP

A date is made to meet again in the future to evaluate the outcomes of the mediation.

Children and young people respond well to visual images and catch phrases which they can quickly refer to when they meet conflict. Slogans such as 'look for a win–win' or 'hands are not for hurting' can be adopted by the children and the adults within the school. The Grace Contrino Abrams Peace Foundation in Miami, USA, have 'Rules for Fighting Fair'. These are:

1　Identify the problem.
2　Focus on the problem.
3　Attack the problem not the person.
4　Listen with an open mind.
5　Treat a person's feelings with respect.
6　Take responsibility for your actions.

They also discuss a series of 'fouls'. Fouls are *not* fighting fair. They include name calling, blaming, sneering, not listening, getting even, bringing up the past, threats, pushing, hitting, put downs, bossing, making excuses, and not taking responsibility. In a conflict situation which is escalating, children can be reminded by peers and adults, 'Is this fighting fair or is it a foul?'

Understanding groups

Sometimes problematic behaviour can arise through the social dynamics of the group. Group relationships go through a development process which includes five stages: forming; storming; norming; performing; dorming (Tuckman, 1965).

In the forming stage, individuals come together and are typically cautious and wary of each other – checking each other out. To be able to work well together (perform), a group has to have a common set of rules (norms); however, before they can reach this stage, they usually go through a phase where the individuals vie for status and power (storm). During this storming stage, power struggles between group members occur, with criticism, manipulation, direct or subtle aggression, and alliances being formed and reformed. Every time group membership changes, the group will return to storming. If the group get stuck at the storming stage, they may scapegoat a member of the group, saying things like: 'If it wasn't for so and so we would be getting on fine.' As teachers or workers, we need to be aware of group dynamics and deliberately assist movement through the storming stage – by using team building activities and developing ground rules (or norms). This will reduce aggressive and disruptive behaviour within the group.

When the task is completed (performed), it is important to acknowledge that the group's work together is done and that it is necessary to move on to a new task, possibly in a new group. Group members benefit from the process of 'closure' in which celebration or affirmation of the group's achievements takes place. This is known as 'dorming' and can take a variety of forms. One essential aspect is that members of the group congratulate one another for the completion of the task and for positive ways in which they worked together. Another is to review group feedback on performance and interpersonal relationships among group members. This is an opportunity for the group to evaluate its accomplishments and reflect on the ways in which members worked together. Questions to consider include:

- What did we do well?
- How could we have worked better?
- What was the best thing about working in this group?
- Which qualities of group members benefited the group?
- Did any factors hinder our group from working well together?
- What would be the best way to end our group?

Successful teams go through the five stages in order (see Table 8.1). If there is failure at any point, there will be a reduction in the group's effectiveness and in the quality of relationships among members of the group. Ineffective groups tend not to move beyond the first two stages.

Cooperative group work teaches the value of respect for others, empathy for the feelings of others, sharing of ideas, and the promotion of cooperative, democratic values. Techniques and strategies include, for example, working jointly on a shared task,

Table 8.1   *Developing effective groups*

Forming (awareness)	Commitment to the task among group members; acceptance of one another; establishing ground rules
Storming (conflict)	Clarification of goals; belonging in the group; listening to one another; managing conflict and disagreement
Norming (cooperation)	Involvement with the task; support for all members; communicating well; offering and receiving constructive feedback
Performing (productivity)	Achievement of goals; pride in collaboration; problem solving; making decisions; doing the task
Dorming (separation)	Recognition that the task was done well; satisfaction in the group process; evaluating performance; reviewing relationships within the group; celebrating and closing.

collaborating on a presentation or role-play, addressing a communal problem using the quality circle method, problem solving in a group, using group resources through the jigsaw method, trust-building exercises, peer conferencing over a difficulty like writing block, class discussions on a shared issue such as bullying. The methods can be adapted to any age group and have been shown to have a direct influence on the emotional climate of the school if they are consistently applied (see Cowie et al., 1994, for a review of cooperative group work strategies in action). Classroom-based research studies give useful insights into ways in which cooperative group work can be most effectively used to foster pro-social attitudes and behaviour at school.

Studies which focus on the way in which cooperative group work is experienced by participants (for example, Cowie and Rudduck, 1990) indicate that children vary widely in their perceptions of the group and in their capacity to negotiate their roles within the group. Some pupils express a feeling of well-being in a group and a sense of responsibility towards the others; they enjoy the opportunity to play an active part in resolving conflicts within the group and in learning from one another. Others remain sceptical about the value of cooperative group work and feel uncomfortable taking part in it. Although they do not actively undermine their groups at the time, when asked for their views they will typically grumble about the experience on the grounds that 'it is a waste of time', 'the soft option' or 'resting time between lessons'. A small but influential proportion of pupils is actively hostile to cooperative group work (Cowie et al., 1994), particularly boys rejected by their peers and those boys and girls who bully others. They report that they dislike group work on the grounds that 'they prefer to work with their friends'. A subtext to this preference is that they are more likely to be racially prejudiced, unsympathetic to children with special needs and intolerant of vulnerable peers. They do not (if boys) like working with girls. The values of cooperation – sharing, supporting others, reflecting on interactions within the group – are not attractive to these children and their uncooperative attitudes regularly cause difficulties within their groups.

Research studies of group process offer helpful guidelines to teachers on how to manage the interpersonal relationships effectively both for task completion and for the enhancement of a cooperative climate in class. Hertz-Lazarowitz (1992) stresses the need to look developmentally at the life of a group and to explore changes which take place over time, since participants are likely to come from a range of different starting points and may well need time to adjust to the norms of a new group. Brown and Palinscar (1989) demonstrate that it is helpful for children regularly to unravel some of the interpersonal processes occurring in the course of group activity. They note that group members commonly adopt a variety of roles – for example, peacemaker, recordkeeper, critic, executor, joker – and find that the roles can be rotated with the right support and training from the teacher. These authors demonstrate that children can be taught the appropriate skills for these roles and recommend that the teacher does not simply leave to chance the allocation of roles within a group.

If the teacher gives children opportunities to work outside friendship groups, supported by appropriate understanding of group processes and with a repertoire of strategies for facilitating groups, then there is a framework for widening their network of social relationships in the classroom. Numerous research studies in many educational contexts provide evidence that we can improve children's capacity to act cooperatively with one another by structuring their classroom experience to enhance peer group interaction As Warden and Christie argue, 'by engaging children in thinking about and discussing the whole spectrum of social behaviour we will help them to develop their social understanding' (1997, p. 87). When teachers give children the opportunity to reflect on the conflicts which inevitably occur in their

everyday lives and to discuss the consequences both of interpersonal conflict and of cooperation, they promote pro-social
behaviour and values in their classrooms on a daily basis. Although we have focused on behaviour management in schools in
this section, the same principles apply to other environments such
as therapeutic groups and home settings.

Tackling individual behaviour

Patterns of individual behaviour are usually considered in terms
of antecedents and consequences: the antecedents are the immediate and wider context in which the behaviour occurs; the
consequences are what follows from it. Classroom layout, noise
levels, appropriateness of task, relationships between teacher or
peers, hunger, teacher response – all sorts of factors influence
behaviour. The following case studies illustrate the complex web
of factors which influence how individuals behave.

Case study

Six-year-old Dune much preferred to be at home than at school. One
day, by accident, he soiled himself at school. The Headteacher made
a huge fuss about this and sent him home. The following day, Dune
soiled himself again – again he was sent home. From then on this
became a regular occurrence; the consequence of his behaviour –
being sent home – was encouraging Dune to maintain his soiling.
Once the Headteacher became aware of this pattern he stopped
sending Dune home, after three occasions the soiling stopped.

Case study

A 14-year-old girl was consistently causing fights within class.
Analysis of the incidents indicated that the fights always occurred
when the girl was sitting near a particular boy. This information was
presented to the girl who explained that he was taunting her subtly
throughout the lessons. He only stopped when she really lost her
temper and responded aggressively. Some mediation work between
the two resolved the situation.

The two case studies above present a simple picture of the
interaction between context and behaviour. Often the relationships are more complex, reflecting not only the influence of the
context on one individual but also the interrelationship between

multiple individuals, their belief systems, their contexts, the social dynamics of the group and the culture of the organization. Watkins (1995) proposes ten important questions for analysing individual behaviour:

- What specific behaviour is causing concern?
- In what situations does the behaviour occur (when/where/ who with)?
- In what situations does the behaviour not occur?
- What happens before the behaviour (a precipitating pattern/ build up/trigger)?
- What follows the behaviour causing concern (something which maintains the behaviour)?
- What skills does the person demonstrate?
- What skills does the person apparently not demonstrate (and how may these be developed)?
- What view does the person have of their behaviour (and what does it mean to them)?
- What view do others have of this person (How has this developed/is it self-fulfilling/can it change)?
- Who is most concerned by this behaviour?

In answering these questions a solution can often be developed – it may become apparent that a consequence is maintaining the behaviour or that it is only happening in certain contexts which can then be changed. Watkins points out that research into very challenging behaviour suggests that each individual probably requires a unique solution. There are no quick fix, easy answers which can be applied universally. Table 8.2 is an example of one teacher's solutions developed through the ten important questions.

Essentially, when trying to intervene in disruptive and aggressive behaviour we have to identify:

1   What is happening (in concrete, measurable terms).
2   Why it is happening (immediate and distant contextual antecedents and consequences).

Having developed a clear understanding of what is happening and why, we can then look for patterns which will help us to know what to do to intervene effectively. As illustrated in Table 8.2, there may be a range of different interventions which collectively will impact on the behaviour. Most interventions will involve altering the antecedents or consequences, including trying

Table 8.2   *Using Watkins's (1995) ten important questions to develop a behaviour action plan*

Important question	Answer	Action
What specific behaviour is causing concern?	Distracts peers by calling out, getting out of seat, hitting, swearing.	
In what situations does the behaviour occur?	When presented with a task involving writing; in a group situation.	Explore why writing such a problem. Structure writing tasks more carefully – break down into manageable steps with clear time goals. Give 'settling down time'. Sit with good role model. Comment on good working behaviour of peers.
In what situations does the behaviour not occur?	In Maths activities; when sitting by self.	Praise and give feedback on good working behaviour in these situations.
What happens before the behaviour?	I get tense because I'm expecting trouble.	Relax! Expect success.
What follows the behaviour?	I get cross; send him out of the class to Headteacher. (Pupil doesn't do the task!)	Stay calm. Keep in class and work with him until he settles down to work.
What skills does the person demonstrate?	?	Look for skills.
What skills doesn't the person demonstrate?	Settling down to work; self-organization; concentration.	Develop programme for teaching these – prompt sheet: 'things I need for writing tasks'; explore strategies for how we concentrate.
What view does the person have of themselves?	?	Ask.
What view do others have?	Class clown.	Point out positive behaviour; establish responsible role.
Who is most concerned by this behaviour?	Me.	Ask for discussion of behaviour management to be put on staff meeting agenda.

to shift the adult's feelings, thoughts and expectations about the 'problem' behaviour.

Some commonly used strategies for encouraging children and young people to change or adapt their behaviour are included in the next section.

Provide a model for appropriate behaviour
When we want to change behaviour, we often have an idea of a behaviour we want to stop. We also have to identify an appropriate alternative – what do we want to happen instead? Once we have identified the preferred alternative behaviour we have to make this explicit to the child or young person through demonstration, work with them to practise it, and point out other people behaving in this way.

Uzzal kicks other children when he wants their attention. His mother will work on him stopping kicking and saying 'Listen to me' instead. As well as practising this through role-play with Uzzal, she comments on other children's behaviours, praising appropriate ways of drawing attention to self – for example, 'Uzzal, Sami said "Watch me!" That's a good way of getting the others to notice him.'

Reinforce desired behaviours
When the child or young person uses the appropriate behaviour, adults and peers can reward or reinforce the behaviour. This does not have to be a physical reward – children and young people can be highly motivated by a positive comment, a nod, a smile. Reward behaviour straight away and be specific about what behaviour is being reinforced, for example: 'Well done, Uzzal, you asked the children to look at you.'

Rewards can include:

- public or private verbal approval
- public or private non-verbal approval
- public or private written approval
- positive report to parent or significant other
- time for an enjoyable activity – staying up late for ten minutes; five minutes free play
- material reward – sticker, small toy, small amount of money.

A physical reward such as time, a token or gift should always be accompanied by verbal and non-verbal praise.

Schools and families often use token systems to reinforce positive behaviour: star charts, marbles in a jar, and so on. The child is rewarded with the agreed token each time they demonstrate the desired behaviour. Sometimes a larger reinforcer is linked to achieving a certain number of tokens – praise from the Head-teacher, a positive letter home, time to play with a favourite toy, etc. Token systems enable both the child and the adults working with the child to see evidence of progress.

'Catch them being good'

It is easy for adults to pay attention to inappropriate behaviour and to ignore more appropriate behaviour. If the child is behaving well, then acknowledge this with a non-verbal or verbal comment. Seize every opportunity to comment on appropriate behaviour – both of the target child and of others. 'It's lovely to see you really listening carefully to the story' or 'Good, playing quietly'. Some parents and teachers agree a 'secret signal' with the child which they use when the child is behaving well, to give them positive feedback about their behaviour. Almost all of us respond well to praise, and will usually do more of whatever behaviour is praised. If you are working with or looking after a child who often misbehaves, go out of your way to notice when they are being good and comment on it.

Do not reinforce inappropriate behaviour

Respond to inappropriate behaviour quietly, firmly and imme-diately. State what is wrong and what the child should do instead. Returning to our example of Uzzal, we might say, 'Uzzal, don't kick – say "Look at me".'

Shouting and scolding loudly can actually reinforce inappropri-ate behaviour and is best avoided. Some people use a 'time out' system to remove negative reinforcement, especially if there are other children around who respond to the inappropriate behav-iour. A 'time out' system should be:

- quick – it should happen immediately after the inappropriate behaviour
- short – it should last only one or two minutes at the most
- neutral – there should be no stimulation, reinforcement or interaction during the time out.

Time out from reinforcement is intended to remove any possible opportunity for reinforcement to occur and is different from time out to calm down. Time out to calm down is useful when a child is angry or upset. This involves the child going out of the situation – to their bedroom, into the corridor and returning themselves when they feel calm and able to continue positively. There are no time or location restrictions on time out to calm down.

Sanction against inappropriate behaviour
All behaviour has consequences – some are more preferable than others. By establishing sanctions with the child before inappropriate behaviour occurs, the child knows the consequences of their actions. This avoids extreme (and often impossible to achieve) sanctions being meted out in an angry moment, such as: 'You are grounded for a month!' or 'You will never go out to play again!'
  Sanctions might include:

- verbal or non-verbal disapproval
- written disapproval
- notice to significant others
- loss of privilege
- time out
- reparation/opposite action.

Involvement of significant others and reparation are powerful sanctions which should be used constructively rather than destructively. O'Connell (1994) has used 'restorative justice' as an effective intervention when children and young people have been involved in extreme acts of aggression and vandalism. O'Connell bases his work on an understanding of the psychology of shame. He asks, 'Why do we *not* do things which we know are wrong?' Often because we do not want the people we care about to be ashamed of us. O'Connell has noted that too often shame is used impersonally and punitively in criminal proceedings and within school-based or home-based sanctions, with little effect on behaviour. He advocates the involvement of significant others in a constructive way, where they demonstrate to the child that their shame arises because they care and love him or her, but not what she or he has done. The child is then supported by those who love him or her to 'put right' whatever wrong has occurred in a way which is acceptable to the person or people affected by the original action. Once reparation is made, the incident is finished.

Monitoring success
Having begun to intervene, it is worthwhile monitoring the incidence of the challenging behaviour. It is unlikely that behaviour change will be immediate and complete, and it is easy for the person desiring change to become disillusioned or despairing when the behaviour re-occurs. It may be that the gaps between

Constructive use of sanctions: notice to significant others and reparation

Wayne was renowned among his classmates for his domineering, aggressive behaviour. On the surface, he seemed popular and always had a crowd of boys around him, but many of his peers were also afraid of him. The other children knew that if you got on the wrong side of Wayne, life could be very unpleasant. So his nasty behaviour was never challenged, and those who suffered at his hands kept silent. Tall and well-dressed, he was the only child of very young parents. His father believed in strict discipline and applied it often; his mother was more lenient and usually consoled him with a present after a family row. When there was no one at home, Wayne would call round to his grandmother who lived on the same estate. She looked forward to his visits and loved to cook him his favourite food for tea. His parents went out a lot in the evenings so were not always there to monitor his activities in the company of his gang. But Wayne knew that he could always rely on his granny to be there for him, even although he would never have admitted this to his friends.

When Leon joined the class from another school in the north, Wayne and his gang took delight in mimicking his accent, laughing at his clothes and hairstyle; the verbal abuse escalated into physical attacks and menacing threats. No one dared to intervene and Leon became increasingly withdrawn and fearful. His parents became concerned since, until this time, he had been an outgoing, happy child. When they questioned him, he said reluctantly that Wayne was regularly 'taxing' him of his lunch money and that he had to pay up for fear of reprisals. They complained to the Headteacher, Mr Naylor. He decided to call in both Wayne and Leon, and their respective families, to see if he could restore a state of justice. Knowing of the important role played by Wayne's grandmother in the life of the family, Mr Naylor asked particularly that she attend the meeting.

Mr Naylor began the meeting by asking Wayne to tell everyone some of the things which he and his friends had done to Leon. Wayne gave a brief account of the teasing and physical aggression. The Headteacher went on to encourage Wayne to tell the group how he had felt at the time and how he felt now. Wayne said that at the time he thought 'it was a laugh' but now he realized that 'he'd gone over the top'. Next Mr Naylor asked first Leon then his family to describe how they felt, both at the time and since. Leon described how he had first been angry at his treatment by his classmates but very soon had begun to doubt himself, becoming more and more afraid of what they would do next. Finally he described lying awake at night picturing over and over again what had happened that day and the increasing dread he felt as the time approached for school each morning. At this point Wayne's dad raised his voice to berate Wayne in a cold threatening manner. Wayne's mum wept and tried to comfort Wayne who, avoiding eye-contact and maintaining a hard expression, angrily brushed her aside. Then the grandmother spoke of her disappointment that her adored grandson could do such things. She stressed how good he had always been with her and how much she looked forward to his visits. As she spoke she looked at Wayne with shock and love mingled in her eyes. Up to this point Wayne had looked away from his family but when his grandmother described her pleasure in his company he looked up at her and suddenly his face reddened and his eyes filled with tears, clearly overwhelmed with shame at her disillusionment with him.

This was the moment for Mr Naylor to intervene, not with retribution but with restorative justice. He reminded everyone that he was not surprised that Wayne's grandmother was shocked and disappointed – he was too because everyone knew that Wayne was actually a kind and pleasant boy who had done some very unpleasant things. Nothing could erase those 'unkind acts' but what they would all be thinking about was how Wayne could make up or put right what he had done wrong. It was important that everyone, and especially Wayne, remembered that although the things he had done were wrong, Wayne was a decent human being who had many strong points and his family could be proud of him. Mr Naylor asked Leon whether there was anything Wayne could do to 'put right' his earlier wrongdoings. Leon thought for a few moments. Hesitantly he suggested, 'Well . . . he could just stop doing it . . . and maybe just, you know, be a bit more friendly.' Mr Naylor turned to Wayne, 'Well, Wayne? What do you think you should do to put this right?' Wayne was much more punishing on himself. As well as 'being mates' with Leon he felt he should be sanctioned by the school, possibly even excluded.

Mr Naylor said that as long as Wayne was truly ashamed of his actions and prepared to do what Leon asked, there was no need for further sanctions. The embarrassment Wayne had so clearly felt at his grandmother's reaction was a strong punishment and would be something Wayne would long remember. The boys and their families agreed how they would make sure things were different in the future and work together to try to develop a more cooperative relationship.

---

occurrences are greater or that the duration of the problematic behaviour is shorter. Without monitoring, such change is easily overlooked or dismissed. Monitoring the change provides evidence that change has occurred and can motivate the people concerned to continue their efforts. Involvement of the child or young person in self-monitoring is beneficial as it increases commitment and responsibility for change and emphasizes self-control.

Maintenance of change

Behaviour management programmes often fail because they are not continued over a reasonable period of time. Once there has been an improvement, everybody tends to return to their previous ways of interacting. Unfortunately, this means that the original contextual influences are likely to be resumed and, therefore, the problems may re-emerge. Once we have discovered how to prevent a behaviour from arising, we have to maintain those changes over time; we have to continue to reward appropriate behaviour and provide direct feedback about inappropriate behaviour, ensuring that we are not inadvertently rewarding the very behaviours we wish to reduce. There are no quick fixes in behaviour management.

Emphasis on self-control

Many of the approaches to behaviour management build upon manipulation of the environment around the child – either in terms of physical setting or the behaviour of adults who work with him or her. It may be easy to assume that behaviour is something which is shaped totally by external forces. This is a dangerous assumption and we encourage an emphasis on active involvement of the child or young person in identifying the problem and finding a solution. Successful behaviour management depends upon self-regulation and control. In any given situation we have a choice of actions, even though we may be influenced to select a particular route. Ultimately, the only person we control is ourselves.

9

TAKING PREVENTATIVE ACTION: DEVELOPING RESILIENCE IN CHILDREN AND YOUNG PEOPLE

> Children, unlike adults, do not have many places where they can operate as a collective group. Adults have factories, work-places, the community in which they live. For children, a primary place for interacting as a group is at school.
>
> (Dalrymple and Hough, 1995, p. 47)

Children and young people who are more resilient when faced with stress and trauma are those who are socially competent, have effective problem-solving skills, are autonomous, and have a sense of purpose and future. Schools and other organizations, parents and families can create an environment which fosters resilience by teaching children and young people these skills. In this final chapter we will consider some of the ways in which this can be achieved.

Creating a caring climate in schools

The importance of having a 'significant other' relationship either within school or at home has been emphasized by the research into effective coping. At school, this is often a teacher but can also be a peer. Establishing a strong pastoral system within the school, one which involves all staff in the development of student social and emotional welfare and enables every student to feel overtly valued, will help to create a caring climate. This can be augmented by peer support networks and a curriculum which encourages mutual respect, cooperation and effective relationship management.

In 1996, The National Commission on Education reported a study of eleven schools that were successful despite significant disadvantages. They noted that these schools which were 'successful against the odds' had a clear philosophy about education shared by all staff. The philosophy was very often an inclusive and optimistic one such as 'all children can succeed' (Maden and Hillman, 1996). This kind of philosophy implies that success in learning relates to effort rather than ability and this has been recognized as an important feature in positive motivation of students (Dweck, 1986). It also emphasizes positive expectations of student success and can contribute to students developing a sense of purpose and future which helps them to cope more effectively with stress. Linking achievement with effort also places a greater emphasis on competency and efficacy – it teaches that we can shape and manage our lives.

Casdagli and Gobey (1990) recommend that schools ensure that all staff understand and can recognize the impact of grief, loss and post-trauma stress on student behaviour. When investigating disruptive behaviour, the possibility that this behaviour is linked to stress and distress should be explored (see Chapter 8).

Part of the preparation for stressful events such as loss and bereavement can be achieved through the curriculum. Although it is difficult to prepare youngsters for catastrophe and disaster, death is as much a part of the life cycle as birth. Many children have experienced the death or loss of a pet, if not a relative. This type of curriculum teaching does not have to focus solely on death – grief and distress can be caused by any change or loss: breakdown of a friendship, moving class, moving school, moving house, divorce, birth of a sibling. This kind of teaching should be embedded throughout the curriculum and will, therefore, require the preparation of teachers who may well have experienced significant loss themselves or find it hard to handle change. In a society which increasingly expects young people entering the workplace to be adaptable, flexible and able to maintain high performance in a context of rapid change, a curriculum focus on effective coping and stress management is preparation for future employment as well as for life.

Developing social competence

The specific behaviours which are deemed to be socially competent will relate to the context within which they occur. Sometimes problems can arise in school because a student may use a coping strategy which is appropriate in one setting but unacceptable in another. Consequently the consortium on the School-based Promotion of Social Competence (1994), which studied the promotion of social competence, defined social competence as: 'life skills for adaptation to diverse ecologies and settings'. A person who is socially competent will realize that different contexts call for different kinds of behaviours. The skills needed to enable a person to be socially perceptive and flexible are fairly universal. They include the following:

- encoding relevant social cues – for example attending to non-verbal language or social norms within any context
- accurate interpretation of encoded social cues – for example taking the other person's perspective, reading intentions, developing empathy
- generating effective solutions to interpersonal problems
- realistically appraising the consequences of behaviour
- behaving in a socially appropriate way – for example, being able to approach and converse with a range of peers and adults, and adopting appropriate tone of voice, posture, language
- displaying a positive sense of self efficacy or competency.

Social situations demand three key tasks: group entry and social approach, relationship maintenance and resolution of conflict (Asher and Taylor, 1981). The core skills have to be applied to each task. In order to develop these core skills the Consortium identified that the key ingredients of effective social programmes included teaching in three areas: emotional, cognitive and behavioural. The specific sub-skills to be taught in each area are listed in Table 9.1.

The consortium points out that teaching programmes to establish these skills need to be long term, with booster sessions built in once the main programme is finished. Involvement of the family, community and school in supporting the programme is an important feature of success.

Linked to social competence is a growing emphasis on the development of 'emotional literacy', particularly marked in North America. To quote Goleman (1996), this emphasis has arisen through recognition of 'the desperate need for lessons in handling emotions, settling disagreements peaceably and just plain getting along' (p. 231). Evidence of increased problems with withdrawal, anxiety, depression, attention and thinking, delinquency and

Table 9.1 *The key ingredients of effective programmes for the development of social competence (Elias and Clabby, 1992)*

Emotional skills	Cognitive skills	Behavioural skills
<ul><li>Identifying and labelling feelings</li><li>Expressing feelings</li><li>Assessing the intensity of feelings</li><li>Managing feelings</li><li>Delaying gratification</li><li>Controlling impulses</li><li>Reducing stress</li><li>Differentiating between feelings and actions</li></ul>	<ul><li>Self talk/self instruction about ways of coping and behaving</li><li>Challenging negative thoughts</li><li>Reading and interpreting social cues</li><li>Setting goals</li><li>Identifying alternative actions and recognizing their consequences</li><li>Understanding the perspectives of others</li><li>Understanding behavioural norms</li><li>A positive attitude towards life</li><li>Having realistic expectations about life</li></ul>	<ul><li>Communicating through eye contact, facial expression, tone of voice, gesture</li><li>Making clear requests</li><li>Eliciting support from others</li><li>Responding effectively to criticism</li><li>Resisting negative influences</li><li>Listening to others</li><li>Helping others</li><li>Participating in positive peer groups</li></ul>

aggression have given impetus to educationalists to include teaching of emotional as well as academic skills. Goleman includes a summary of the main components of the 'Self Science Curriculum' – some of which overlaps with the social competence curriculum outlined in Table 8.1 – and provides examples of the programme being used in North American schools. The components are as follows:

- **Self awareness**: self-monitoring and recognition of feelings; building a vocabulary of feelings; making links between thoughts, feelings and behaviour
- **Personal decision making**: self-monitoring of actions and recognition of their consequences; distinguishing between thought-led and feeling-led decisions
- **Managing feelings**: self-monitoring of 'self talk'; challenging negative self-messages; recognizing triggers for strong feelings; finding ways of handling fears, anxieties, anger, sadness
- **Handling stress**: self-monitoring for signs of stress, recognition of sources of stress, learning to use relaxation methods

- **Empathy**: understanding others' feelings and concerns; recognizing that different people have different perspectives and trying to work these out
- **Communications**: talking about feelings, developing listening and question asking skills, differentiating between what someone actually says and does, and your interpretations or judgements of this; using 'I' messages and other assertive language; avoiding blame language
- **Self-disclosure**: building trust into a relationship, valuing and respecting openness; judging when it is appropriate to talk about personal feelings
- **Insight**: self-monitoring and recognition of patterns in emotional reactions in self and others
- **Self-acceptance and positive attribution**: identifying links between effort and achievement, acknowledging success, feeling pride and having a positive view of self, recognizing strengths and weaknesses, being able to laugh at self
- **Personal responsibility**: taking responsibility for self-management; recognizing consequences of actions and decisions; accepting feelings and moods; persisting to achieve goals and commitments
- **Assertiveness**: stating your concerns and feelings without anger or passivity, with mutual respect for self and others
- **Group dynamics**: understanding how groups work; self-monitoring of own contribution to group effectiveness; cooperation and collaboration, leading and following
- **Conflict resolution**: understanding the difference between need and want, using a 'win–win' model for negotiating solutions.

The impact of emotional literacy or social competence programmes have been documented through evaluation studies (for example, Elias and Clabby, 1992; Greenberg et al., 1995). Outcomes include increases in:

- accurate interpretation of social situations and selection of appropriate behaviours
- awareness of own and other's feelings
- understanding of consequence of behaviour
- self-esteem
- pro-social behaviour
- effective management of change
- self-control.

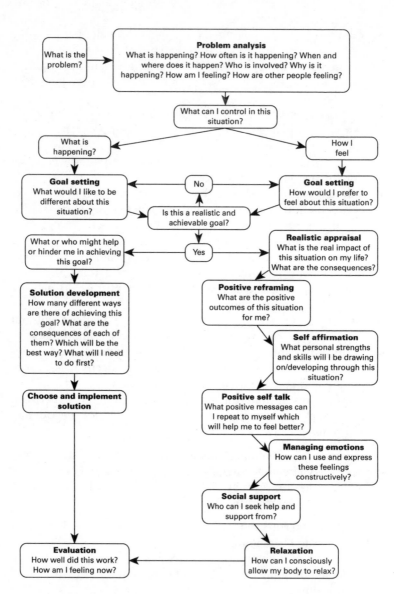

Figure 9.1   *Decision-making process for effective coping*

Developing effective coping

Coping strategies fall into two groups: problem-focused coping strategies, which aim to find a solution to the situation or change something about the situation which will make it less stressful; and emotion-focused coping strategies, which do not alter the situation but help the individual to feel better about it. A key skill in effective coping is assessing the situation and deciding which type of response is most appropriate. If a problem-focused strategy is called for, the child or young person will engage in a step-by-step problem solving process. This will include problem identification and analysis: goal setting; and generation, implementation and evaluation of a solution. If the problem is totally out of the individual's control, then emotion-focused coping is required. Emotion-focused coping involves changing how you feel or think about the situation. This can be achieved through realistic evaluation of the consequences of the problem; positive reframing of the situation; positive affirmation of self; appropriate expression of emotion; and relaxation. In many stressful situations, both coping responses are appropriate and can be used simultaneously. The flow diagram in Figure 9.1 illustrates decision-making for effective coping.

By developing a resilient youth we equip them for the ups and downs of life. If we match that with a willingness to take time to listen well when they are experiencing trauma or crisis, then they are more likely to cope effectively. Making a difference is something we can all achieve and we can do it through using everyday skills of listening, talking, drawing, playing, making music. There are special therapeutic approaches which also help but it is within us all to help. We leave you with an anonymous story.

> One day a young man was walking along a beach. He came across an older man picking up starfish and throwing them back into the sea.
> 'What are you doing, old man?' he asked.
> 'When the sun falls on the starfish they die. I throw them back so they will live.'
> 'But look around, old man, there are thousands of starfish here. How can you hope to make a difference?'
> The old man looked down at the small starfish in his hand. As he threw it into the sea he said, 'I make a difference to this one.'

References

Abrams, R. (1992) *When Parents Die*. London: Charles Letts.

Adcock, M. and White, R. (eds) (1985) *Good-enough Parenting: a Framework for Assessment*. British Agency for Fostering and Adoption.

Adler, P.A. and Adler, P. (1995) 'Dynamics of inclusion and exclusion in pre-adolescent cliques', *Social Psychology Quarterly*, 58(3): 145–62.

Agras, W.S., Chapin, N.H. and Oliveau, D.C. (1972) 'The natural history of phobias: course and prognosis', *Archives of General Psychiatry*, 26: 315–17.

Ahmad, Y., Whitney, I. and Smith, P.K. (1991) 'A survey service for schools on bully/victim problems', in P.K. Smith and D.A Thompson (eds), *Practical Approaches to Bullying*. London: David Fulton.

Applebee, A.N. (1978) *The Child's Conception of Story*. Chicago: Chicago University Press.

Asher, S.R. and Taylor, A.R. (1981) 'Social outcomes of mainstreaming: sociometric assessment and beyond', *Exceptional Children Quarterly*, 1: 13–30.

Balding, J., Regis, D., Wise, A., Bish, D. and Muirden, J. (1996) *Bully Off: Young People that Fear going to School*. Exeter: Schools Health Education Unit.

Barrett, H. and Jones, D. (1997) 'Troubles of anger', in V. Varma (ed.), *Troubles of Children and Adolescents*. London: Jessica Kingsley.

Barton, M.L. and Zeanah, C.H. (1990) 'Stress in the pre-school years', in L. Eugene Arnold (ed.), *Childhood Stress*. New York: John Wiley.

Benson, G. (1995) 'Hypnosis as a therapeutic medium', *Educational and Child Psychology*, 12(4): 25–33.

Björkvist, K., Lagerspetz, K.M.J. and Kaukiainen, A. (1992) 'Do girls manipulate and boys fight? Developmental trends in regard to direct and indirect aggression', *Aggressive Behavior*, 18: 117–27.

Björkqvist, K., Osterman, K. and Lagerspetz, K. (1994) 'Sex differences in covert aggression amongst adults', *Aggressive Behaviour*, 20: 27–33.

Block, J.H. and Block, J.H. (1980) 'The role of ego control and ego resiliency in the organisation of behaviour', in W.A. Collins (ed.), *Development of Cognition, Affect and Social Relations*. The Minnesota symposia on child psychology (Vol. 13). Hillsdale, NJ: Lawrence Erlbaum Associates.

Block, J.H. and Gjerde, P.F. (1986) 'Early antecedents of ego-resiliency in late adolescence'. Paper presented at the American Psychological Association meeting, Washington, DC.

Boulton, M. and Underwood, K. (1992) 'Bully/victim problems among middle school children', *British Journal of Educational Psychology*, 62: 73–87.

Bourgault, G. (1991) 'Peer support in high schools: a programme to complement pastoral care strategies', *Pastoral Care*, 10(1): 25–7.

Bowlby, J. (1969) *Attachment and Loss: Attachment*. New York: Basic Books.

Branwhite, T. (1994) 'Bullying and student distress: the tip of the iceberg', *Educational and Child Psychology*, 14(1): 59–71.

Breakwell, G., Fife-Shaw, C. and Devereaux, J.B. (1988) 'The relationship of self esteem and attributional style to young people's worries', *The Journal of Psychology*, 122(3): 207–15.

Bretherton, I. (1990) 'Open communication and internal working models: their role in the development of attachment relationships', in R.A. Thompson (ed.), *Socioemotional Development*. Nebraska Symposium on Motivation 1988. Lincoln: University of Nebraska Press.

Bretherton, I. (1996) 'Internal working models of attachment relationships as related to resilient coping', in G.G. Noam and K.W. Fisher (eds), *Development and Vulnerability in Close Relationships*. Mahwah, NJ: Lawrence Erlbaum Associates.

Brighouse, T. (1993) 'Management of curriculum and teaching methods and pupils' behaviour in school', in Ved P. Varma (ed.), *Management of Behaviour in Schools*. Harlow: Longman.

British Association for Counselling (BAC) (1995) *Guidelines for Counsellors in Schools*. Rugby: BAC.

Britton, J. (1977) 'The role of fantasy', in M. Meek, G. Barton and A. Warlow (eds), *The Cool Web*. London: Bodley Head.

Bronfenbrenner, U. (1979) *The Ecology of Human Development*. Cambridge, MA: Harvard University Press.

Bronfenbrenner, U. and Ceci, S.J. (1994) 'Nature-nurture reconceptualized in developmental perspective: a bioecological model', *Psychological Review*, 10(4): 568–86.

Brown, A.I. and Palinscar, A.S. (1989) 'Guided, cooperative learning and individual knowledge acquisition', in L.B. Resnick (ed.), *Knowing, Learning and Instruction*. Hillsdale, NJ: Lawrence Erlbaum.

Bruner, J.S. (1990) *Acts of Meaning*. Cambridge, MA: Harvard University Press.

Bull, S.L. and Solity, J.E. (1989) *Classroom Management: Principles to Practice*. London: Routledge.

Burman, E. (1996) 'Local, global or globalised? Child development and international children's rights legislation', *Childhood*, 3(1): 45–66.

Cairns, E. (1994) 'Children and political violence', *International Journal of Behavioral Development*, 17(4): 669–74.

Cameron, R.J., Gersch, I., M'Gadzah, H. and Moyse, S. (1995) 'Educational psychologists and post-trauma stress management', *Educational and Child Psychology*, 12(3): 2–21.

Campbell, A. (1993) *Out of Control: Men, Women and Aggression*. London: Harper Collins.

Cantacuzino, M. (1997) 'When time is the only healer', The *Guardian*, 3 September, pp. 8–9.

Carr, R. (1994) 'Peer helping in Canada', *Peer Counselling Journal*, 11(1): 6–9.

Carr, R. and Saunders, D. (1980) *Peer Counselling Starter Kit*. Victoria, BC: Peer Counselling Project, University of Victoria.

Casdagli, P. and Gobey, F. (1990) *Only Playing Miss*. Stoke-on-Trent: Trentham Books.

Cassidy, J. (1988) 'The self as related to child–mother attachment at six', *Child Development*, 59: 121–34.

Chapman, R. (1997) 'When time is the only healer', The *Guardian*, 3 September, pp. 8–9.

Charlton, T. and David, K. (1997) 'Orchestrating success in personal, social and educational areas: using peer support', *Pastoral Care in Education*, March, pp. 22–9.

Children's Rights Development Unit (CRDU) (1993) *The United Nations Convention on the Rights of the Child*. London: UNICEF/Gulbenkian/UNA.

Children's Rights Development Unit (CRDU) (1994) *UK Agenda for Children*. CRDU.

Cohen, L.H. Burt, C.E. and Bjorck, J.P. (1987) 'Life stress and adjustment: effects of life events experienced by young adolescents and their parents', *Developmental Psychology*, 23(4): 583–92.

Coleman, J. and Warren-Adamson, C. (1992) *Youth Policy in the 1980s*. London: Routledge.

Compas, B.E. (1987) 'Coping with stress during childhood and adolescence', *Psychological Bulletin*, 101(3): 393–403.

Compas, B.E. and Phares, V. (1991) 'Stress during childhood and adolescence: sources of risk and vulnerability', in E.M. Cummings, A.L. Greene and K.H. Karraker (eds), *Life Span Developmental Psychology: Perspectives on Stress and Coping*. Hillsdale, NJ: Lawrence Erlbaum Associates.

Compas, B.E., Malcarne, V.L. and Fondacaro, K.M. (1988) 'Coping with stressful events in older children and young adolescents', *Journal of Consulting and Clinical Psychology*, 56(3): 405–411.

Compas, B.E., Orosan, P.G. and Grant, K.E. (1993) 'Adolescent stress and coping: implications for psychopathology during adolescence', *Journal of Adolescence*, 16: 331–49.

Compas, B.E., Banez, G.A., Malcarne, V. and Worsham, N. (1991) 'Perceived control and coping with stress: a developmental perspective', *Journal of Social Issues*, 47(4): 23–34.

Conger, R.D., Xiaojia, G., Elder, G.H., Lorenz, F.O. and Simons, R.L. (1994) 'Economic stress, coercive family process and developmental problems of adolescents', *Child Development*, 65: 541–61.

Conn, C. (1997) 'Dramatherapy and schools', *Young Minds*, 30: 14–17.

The consortium on the School-based Promotion of Social Competence (1994) 'The school based promotion of social competence: theory, research, practice and policy', in R.J. Haggerty, L.R. Sherrod, N. Garmezy and M. Rutter (eds), *Stress, Risk and Resilience in Children and Adolescents: Processes, Mechanisms and Interventions*. Cambridge: Cambridge University Press.

Cowie, H. (in press 1998) 'Perspectives of teachers and pupils on the experience of peer support against bullying', *Educational Research and Evaluation*.

Cowie, H. and Olafsson, R. (in submission) 'The role of peer support in helping the victims of bullying', *Journal of Medical Psychology*.

Cowie, H. and Pecherek, A. (1994) *Counselling: Approaches and Issues in Education*. London: David Fulton.

Cowie, H. and Rudduck, J. (1990) *Cooperative Group Work: Traditions and Transitions*. London: BP Educational Services.

Cowie, H. and Sharp, S. (eds) (1996) *Peer Counselling in Schools: a Time to Listen*. London: David Fulton.

Cowie, H., Smith, P.K., Boulton, M. and Laver, R. (1994) *Cooperation in the Multi-ethnic Classroom*. London: David Fulton.

Cox (1978) *Stress*. Basingstoke: Macmillan Education.

Crittenden, P. (1992) 'Treatment of anxious attachment in infancy and early childhood', *Development and Psychopathology*, 4: 575–602.

Curry, J.F., Miller, Y., Waugh, S. and Anderson, W.B. (1992) 'Coping responses in depressed, socially maladjusted and suicidal adolescents', *Psychological Reports*, 71: 80–2.

Dale, R.R. (1991) 'Mixed versus single-sex schools: the social aspect of bullying', in M. Elliott (ed.), *Bullying: a Practical Guide to Coping in Schools*. Harlow: Longman.

Dalley, T. (1993) 'Art psychotherapy groups', in N. Dwivedi (ed.), *Groupwork with Children and Adolescents*. London: Jessica Kingsley.

Dalrymple, J. and Hough, J. (1995) *Having a Voice: an Exploration of Children's Rights and Advocacy*. Birmingham: Venture Press.

Demetriades, A. (1996) 'Children of the storm: peer partnership', in H. Cowie and S. Sharp (eds), *Peer Counselling in School: a Time to Listen*. London: David Fulton.

Dent, A., Condom, L., Blair, P. and Fleming, P. (1996) 'A study of bereavement care after a sudden and unexpected death', *Archives of Disease in Childhood*, 74: 522–6.

De Rosier, M.E., Cillessen, A.H.N., Coie, J.D. and Dodge, K.A. (1994) 'Group social context and children's aggressive behaviour', *Child Development*, 65: 1068–79.

DES (1989) *Discipline in Schools: Report of the Committee Chaired by Lord Elton*. London: HMSO.

DFE (1992) Government White Paper, *Choice and Diversity: a New Framework for Schools*. London: HMSO.

Docking, J. (1993) 'The management of behaviour in primary schools', in Ved P. Varma (ed.), *Management of Behaviour in Schools*. Harlow: Longman.

DuBois, D.L., Felner, R.D., Brand, S., Adan, A.M. and Evans, E.G. (1992) 'A prospective study of life stress, social support and adaptation in early adolescence', *Child Development*, 63: 542–57.

Dunn, J. (1988) *The Beginnings of Social Understanding*. Oxford: Basil Blackwell.

Dweck, C. (1986) 'Motivational processes affect learning', *American Psychologist*, 41: 1040–8.

Dwivedi, N. (1993) *Groupwork with Children and Adolescents*. London: Jessica Kingsley.

Dyregrov, A. (1991) *Grief in Children: a Handbook for Adults*. London: Jessica Kingsley.

Eaton, M.T., Peterson, M.H. and Davis, J.A. (1981) 'Psychological factors affecting physical conditions', in M. Eaton, M.H. Peterson and J.A. Davis (eds), *Psychiatry*. Garden City, NY: Medical Examination Publishing Company.

Elias, M.J. and Clabby, J.F. (1992) *Building Social Problem Solving Skills: Guidelines from a School Based Programme*. New York: Institute for Rational Living.

Ellis, A. (1970) *The Essence of Rational Psychotherapy: a Comprehensive Approach to Treatment*. New York: Institute for Rational Living.

Emery, R.E. and Forehand, R. (1994) 'Parental divorce and children's well-being: a focus on resilience', in R.J. Haggerty, L.R. Sherrod, N. Garmezy and M. Rutter (eds), *Stress, Risk and Resilience in Children and Adolescents: Processes, Mechanisms and Interventions*. Cambridge: Cambridge University Press.

Engel, S. (1995) *The Stories Children Tell*. York: W.H. Freeman and Co.

Erickson, M.F., Egeland, B. and Sroufe, L. A. (1985) 'The relationship between quality of attachment and behavior problems in preschool in a high-risk sample', in I. Bretherton and E. Waters (eds), *Growing Points in Attachment Theory and Research. Monographs of the Society for Research in Child Development*, 50 (1–2, Serial No 209): 147–86.

Erwin, P. (1993) *Friendship and Peer Relations in Children*. Chichester: Wiley.

Eslea, M. and Smith, P.K. (1996) 'If anybody hits you you hit them back! Parent and pupil attitudes towards bullying in primary schools'. Paper presented at the 14th meeting of the ISSBD Quebec, August 1996.

Felner, R.D., Brand, S., DuBois, D.L., Adan, A.M., Mulhall, P.F. and Evans, E.G. (1995) 'Socio-economic disadvantage, proximal environmental experiences and socioemotional and academic adjustment in early adolescence: investigation of a mediated effects model', *Child Development*, 66: 774–92.

Freeman, A. (1986) 'Coping in schools', unpublished dissertation: University of Sheffield.

Freud, A. and Dann, S. (1951) 'An experiment in group upbringing', *Psychoanalytic Study of the Child*, 6: 127–68.

Frydenberg, E. (1997) *Adolescent Coping*. London: Routledge.

Gardner, H. (1993) *The Unschooled Mind*. London: Fontana.

Garmezy, N. and Masten, A. (1991) 'The protective role of competence indicators in children at risk', in E.M. Cummings, A.L. Greene and K.H. Karraker (eds), *Life Span Developmental Psychology: Perspectives on Stress and Coping*. Hillsdale, NJ: Lawrence Erlbaum Associates.

Garmezy, N. and Rutter, M. (eds) (1983) *Stress, Coping and Development in Children*. New York: McGraw-Hill.

Garton, A.F. and Pratt, C. (1995) 'Stress and self concept in 10 to 15 year olds', *Journal of Adolescence*, 18: 625–40.

Gersie, A. (1991) *Story-making in Bereavement*. London: Jessica Kingsley.

Gibson-Cline, J. (1996) *Adolescence – from Crisis to Coping: a Thirteen Nation Study*. Oxford: Butterworth-Heinemann.

Goleman, E. (1996) *Emotional Intelligence*. London: Bloomsbury.

Gore, S. and Colton, M. (1991) 'Gender, stress and distress: social-relational influences', in J. Eckenrode (ed.), *The Social Context of Coping*. New York: Plenum Press.

Gore, S. and Eckenrode, J. (1994) 'Context and process in research on risk and resilience', in R.J. Haggerty, L.R. Sherrod, N. Garmezy and M. Rutter (eds), *Stress, Risk and Resilience in Children and Adolescents: Processes, Mechanisms and Interventions*. Cambridge: Cambridge University Press.

Greenberg, M.T., Kusche, C.A., Cooke, E.T. and Quamma, J.P. (1995) 'Promoting emotional competence in school aged children: the effects of the PATHS curriculum', *Development and Psychopathology*, 7: 7–16.

Guggenbhul, A. (1991) 'Tales and fiction', *School Psychology International*, 12: 7–16.

Hardy, B. (1977) 'Narrative as a primary act of mind', in M. Meek, G. Barton and A. Warlow (eds), *The Cool Web*. London: Bodley Head.

Harwood, R., Miller, J. and Irizarry, N. (1995) *Culture and Attachment*. New York: The Guilford Press.

Haselager, G.J.T. and Van Lieshout, C.F.M. (1992) 'Social and affective adjustment of self and peer reported victims about bullies'. Paper presented at the 5th European Conference on Developmental Psychology, Seville.

Hayworth, M. (1989) 'Grief in children', in B. Ward (ed.), *Good Grief: Exploring Feelings, Loss and Death with Under 11s*. Good Grief, 19 Bawtree Road, Uxbridge, Middx UB8 1PT.

Hazler, R. (1996) 'Bystanders: an overlooked factor in peer on peer abuse', *The Journal for the Professional Counselor*, 11(2): 11–21.

Hendren, R.L. (1990) 'Stress in adolescence', in L. Eugene Arnold (ed.), *Childhood Stress*. New York: John Wiley.

Henry, J.P. (1980) 'Present concepts of stress theory', in E. Ursdin, R. Kvetnansky and I.J. Copin (eds), *Catecholemines and Stress*. New York: Elsevier.

Hershberger, S.L. and D'Augelli, A.R. (1995) 'The impact of victimization on the mental health and suicidality of lesbian, gay and bisexual youth', *Developmental Psychology*, 31: 65–74.

Hertz-Lazarowitz, R. (1992) 'Understanding interactive behaviors: looking at six mirrors of the classroom', in R. Herz-Lazarowitz and N. Miller (eds), *Interaction in Cooperative Groups*. Cambridge: Cambridge University Press.

HMSO (1989) *The Children Act*. London: HMSO.

Hojat, M. (1997) 'The UN Convention on the rights of the child: lost in the clash of adverse opinions', *American Psychologist*, 52(12): 1384.

Holmes, T.H. and Rahe, R.H. (1967) 'The social readjustment rating scale', *Journal of Psychosomatic Research*, 11: 213–18.

Hoover, J.H. (1996) 'Why I study bullying', *Journal of Emotional and Behavioral Problems*, 5(1): 10–11.

Hoover, J.H., Oliver, R. and Hazler, R. (1992) 'Bullying: perceptions of adolescent victims in the mid-western USA', *School Psychology International*, 13: 5–16.

Houghton, K. (1996) 'Critical incidents involving schoolchildren: research update', *Educational and Child Psychology*, 13(3): 59–75.

Hunter, J. and Schaecher, J. (1987) 'Stresses on lesbian and gay adolescents in schools', *Social Work in Education*, 9: 180–190.

James, J., Charlton, T., Leo, E. and Indoe, D. (1991) 'A peer to listen', *Support for Learning*, 6(4): 165–9.

Jennings, S. (1986) *Creative Drama in Groupwork*. Bicester: Winslow Press.

Kaye, P.G. and Webb, A. (1996) 'A little help from my friends: a secondary school peer support programme', *Pastoral Care in Education*, 14(2): 23–5.

Kimchi, J. and Schaffner, B. (1990) 'Childhood protective factors and stress risk', in L. Eugene Arnold (ed.), *Childhood Stress*. New York: John Wiley.

King, N.J., Hamilton, D.I. and Ollendick, T.H. (1994) *Children's Phobias: a Behavioural Perspective*. Chichester: John Wiley.

Kirkwood, N. (1989) 'A child's questions about death', in B. Ward, *Good Grief*. Luton: White Crescent Press.

Konet, R. (1991) 'Peer helpers in the middle school', *Middle School Journal*, September: 13–16.

La Fontaine, J. (1991) *Bullying: the Child's View*. London: Calouste Gulbenkian Foundation.

Lagerspetz, K.M.J., Björkqvist, K., Berts, M. and King, E. (1982) 'Group aggression among school children in three schools', *Scandinavian Journal of Psychology*, 23: 45–52.

Lazarus, A.A. and Abramovitz, A. (1962) 'The use of emotive imagery in the treatment of children's phobias', *Journal of Mental Science*, 108: 191–5.

Lendrum, S. and Syme, G. (1992) *Gift of Tears*. London: Routledge.

Lloyd, G. (1997) 'Can the law support children's rights in schools in Scotland and prevent the development of a climate of blame?', *Pastoral Care in Education*, September 13–16.

MacLeod, M. and Morris, S. (1996) *Why Me?* London: ChildLine.

Maden, M. and Hillman, J. (1996) 'Lessons in success'. In National Commission on Education, *Success against the Odds*. London: Routledge.

Main, M. and Cassidy, J. (1988) 'Categories of response to reunion with the parent at age 6: predictable from infant classifications and stable over a 1-month period', *Developmental Psychology*, 24(3): 415–26.

Maines, B. and Robinson, G. (1997) *Crying for Help*. Bristol: Lucky Duck Publishing.

Marks, I.M. and Gelder, M.G. (1966) 'Different ages of onset in varieties of phobia', *American Journal of Psychiatry*, 123: 218–21.

Mason, J.W. (1975) 'Emotions as reflected in patterns of endocrine integration', in L. Levi (ed.), *Emotions: their Parameters and Measurement*. New York: Raven.

Mellor, A. (1990) *Bullying in Scottish Secondary Schools*. Edinburgh: Scottish Council for Research in Education.

Menesini, E., Fonzi, A. and Genta, M.-L. (1996) 'Bullying behaviour and attitudes among Italian school children'. Paper presented at the European Congress on Educational Research (ECER), Seville, September.

Mental Health Foundation (1993) *Mental Illness – The Fundamental Facts*. London: Mental Health Foundation.

Miller, A. (1994) *Pupil Behaviour and Teacher Culture*. London: Cassell.

Mooij, T. (1993) 'Working towards understanding and prevention in The Netherlands', in D.P. Tattum (ed.), *Understanding and Managing Bullying*. Oxford: Heinemann Educational.

Morita, Y. (1996) 'Bullying as a contemporary problem', *Prospects*, 26(2): 311–329.

Naylor, P. and Cowie, H. (forthcoming) 'Peer support systems as a challenge to school bullying: experiences and perspectives of teachers and pupils, *Journal of Adolescence*.

Neary, A. and Joseph, S. (1994) 'Peer victimisation and its relationship to self concept and depression among schoolgirls', *Personality and Individual Differences*, 16(1): 183–6.

Newman, M., Black, D. and Harris-Hendriks, J. (1997) 'Victims of disaster, war, violence or homicide: psychological effects on siblings', *Child Psychology and Psychiatry Review*, 2(4): 140–9.

Newton, C., Taylor, G. and Wilson, D. (1996) 'Circles of friends: an inclusive approach to meeting emotional and behavioural needs', *Educational Psychology in Practice*, 11(4): 41–8.

Norman, P., Foot, M., Gregor, A. and Turner, J. (1997) 'Guidelines for dealing with a critical incident'. Buckinghamshire Educational Psychology Service Report.

O'Connell, T. (1994) 'Family conferencing'. Unpublished manual.

Olah, A. (1995) 'Coping strategies among adolescents: a cross cultural study', *Journal of Adolescence*, 18: 491–512.

Ollendick, T.H., Matson, J.L. and Helsel, W.J. (1985) 'Fears in children and adolescents: normative data', *Behaviour Research and Therapy*, 23: 465–7.

Olweus, D. (1978) *Aggression in Schools. Bullies and Whipping Boys*. Washington, DC: Hemisphere Press.

Olweus, D. (1980) 'Familial and temperamental determinants of aggressive behavior in adolescent boys: a causal analysis', *Child Development*, 16: 644–60.

Olweus, D. (1991) 'Bully/victims problems among school children in Scandinavia', in J.P. Myklebust and R. Ommundsen (eds), *Psykologprofesjonen mot ar 2000*. Oslo: Universitetsforlaget.

Olweus, D. (1993) *Bullying at School*. Oxford: Basil Blackwell.

O'Moore, A.M. and Hillery, B. (1989) 'Bullying in Dublin schools', *Irish Journal of Psychology*, 10: 426–41.

Overholser, J.C. (1992) 'Sense of humour when coping with life stress', *Personality and Individual Differences*, 13(7): 799–804.

Pearlin, L.I. (1991) 'The study of coping: an overview of problems and directions', in J. Eckenrode (ed.), *The Social Context of Coping*. New York: Plenum Press.

Pepler, D. (1996) 'A peek behind the fence: what we have learned about bullying'. Paper presented at the conference *Putting the Brakes on Violence*, York University, Toronto, August 1996.

Pepler, D., Craig, W., Ziegler, S. and Charach, A. (1993) 'Understanding and managing bullying', in D. Tattum (ed.), *Understanding and Managing Bullying*. Oxford: Heinemann (pp. 76–91).

Pervin, K. and Turner, A. (1994) 'An investigation into staff and pupil knowledge, attitudes and beliefs about bullying in inner-city schools', *Pastoral Care in Education*, 13(3): 14–19.

Pikas, A. (1989) 'A pure concept of mobbing gives the best results for treatment', *School Psychology International*, 10: 95–104.

Plancherel, B. and Bolignini, M. (1995) 'Coping and mental health in early adolescence', *Journal of Adolescence*, 18: 459–74.

Protherough, R. (1983) *Developing Response to Fiction*. Milton Keynes: Open University Press.

Pryor-Brown, L., Cowen, E.L., Hightower, A.D. and Lofyczewski, B.S. (1986) 'Demographic differences among children in judging and experiencing specific stressful life events', *The Journal of Special Education*, 20: 339–45.

Quarmby, D. (1993) 'Peer counselling with bereaved adolescents', *British Journal of Guidance and Counselling*, 21(2): 196–211.

Reid, K. (1989) 'Bullying and persistent school absenteeism', in D. Tattum and D. Lane (eds), *Bullying in Schools*. Stoke on Trent: Trentham Books.

Resnick, G. (1993) *Manual for the Administration, Coding and Interpretation of the Separation Anxiety Test for 11 to 14 Year Olds*. Rockville, MD: Westat.

Rice, K.G., Herman, M.A.and Peterson, A.C. (1993) 'Coping with challenge in adolescence: a conceptual model and psycho-educational intervention', *Journal of Adolescence*, 16: 235–51.

Rigby, K. (1996) *Bullying in Australian Schools – and What to Do About It*. Melbourne: ACER.

Rigby, K. (1997) 'What children tell us about bullying in schools', *Children Australia*, 22(2): 28–34.

Rigby, K. and Slee, P. (1991) 'Bullying among Australian school children: reported behaviour and attitudes to victims', *Journal of Social Psychology*, 131: 615–27.

Rivers, I. (1997a) 'The long-term impact of peer victimisation in adolescence upon the well-being of lesbian, gay and bisexual adults'. Paper presented at the Fifth European Congress of Psychology, University College Dublin, Ireland, July.

Rivers, I. (1997b) 'Violence against lesbian and gay youth and its impact', in M. Schneider (ed.), *Pride and Prejudice: Working with Lesbian, Gay and Bisexual Youth*. Toronto: Central Toronto Youth Services (pp. 31–48).

Robertson, J. (1952) *A Two-year-old goes to Hospital* (Film). London: Tavistock.

Robertson, J. and Robertson, J. (1972) 'Young children in brief separations', in R.K. Essler et al. (eds), *The Psychoanalytic Study of the Child*, Vol. 26. New Haven, CT: Yale University Press.

Roland, E. (1989) 'Bullying: the Scandinavian research tradition', in D.P. Tattum and D. Lane (eds), *Bullying in Schools*. Stoke-on-Trent: Trentham Books.

Roland, E. (1993) 'Bullying: a developing tradition of research and management', in D. Tattum (ed.), *Understanding and Managing Bullying*. Oxford: Heinemann Educational.

Rossman, B.B.R. (1992) 'School age children's perceptions of coping with distress: strategies for emotion regulation and the moderation of adjustment', *Journal of Child Psychology and Psychiatry*, 8: 1373–97.

Rubin, Z. (1982) 'Children without friends', in L.A. Peplau and D. Perlman (eds), *Loneliness: a Sourcebook of Current Theory, Research and Therapy*. New York: John Wiley.

Rutter, M. (1994) 'Stress research: accomplishments and tasks ahead', in R.J. Haggerty, L.R. Sherrod, N. Garmezy and M. Rutter (eds), *Stress, Risk and Resilience in Children and Adolescents: Processes, Mechanisms and Interventions*. Cambridge: Cambridge University Press.

Rutter, M. (1998) 'Developmental catch-up, and deficit following adoption after severe global early privation', *Journal of Child Psychology and Psychiatry*, 39(4): 465–76.

Ryan, N.M. (1989) 'Identification of children's coping strategies from the school-agers' perspective', *Research in Nursing and Health*, 12: 111–22.

Ryan-Wenger, N.M. (1990) 'Children's psychosomatic responses to stress', in L. Eugene Arnold (ed.), *Childhood Stress*. New York: John Wiley.

Safran, J.S. and Safran, S.P. (1985) 'A developmental view of children's behavioral tolerance', *Behavioral Disorders*, 10(2): 87–94.

Salmivalli, C., Lagerspetz, K., Björkqvist, K., Osterman, K. and Kaukiainen, A. (1996) 'Bullying as a group process: participant roles and their relations to social status within the group', *Aggressive Behaviour*, 22(1): 1–15.

Scarlett, G. and Wolf, D. (1979) 'When it's only make-believe: the construction of a boundary between fantasy and reality in story-telling', in E. Winner and H. Gardner (eds), *Fact, Fiction and Fantasy in Childhood*. San Francisco: Jossey-Bass.

Schulman, S. (1993) 'Close relationships and coping behaviour in adolescence', *Journal of Adolescence*, 16: 267–84.

Sears, S.J. and Milburn, J. (1990) 'School age stress', in L. Eugene Arnold (ed.), *Childhood Stress*. New York: John Wiley.

Seiffge-Krenke, I. (1993) 'Coping behaviour in normal and clinical samples: more similarities than differences?', *Journal of Adolescence*, 16: 285–304.

Seligman, M. and Hager, J. (eds) (1972) *Biological Boundaries of Learning*. New York: Appleton Century Crofts.

Sharp, S. (1995) 'How much does bullying hurt? The effects of bullying on the personal well-being and educational progress of secondary aged students', *Educational and Child Psychology*, 12, 81–8.

Sharp, S. and Cowie, H. (1994) 'Tackling bullying through the curriculum', in P.K. Smith and S. Sharp (eds), *School Bullying: Insights and Perspectives*, London: Routledge.

Sharp, S. and Thompson, D. (1992) 'Sources of stress: a contrast between pupil perspectives and pastoral teachers' perspectives', *School Psychology International*, 13: 229–42.

Sharp, S. and Thompson, D. (1994) 'The role of whole school policies in tackling bullying in schools', in P.K. Smith and S. Sharp (eds), *School Bullying: Insights and Perspectives*, London: Routledge.

Sharp, S., Sellors, A. and Cowie, H. (1994) 'Time to listen: setting up a peer counselling service to help tackle the problem of bullying in schools', *Pastoral Care in Education*, 12(2): 3–6.

Shorter Oxford English Dictionary (1983). Oxford: Oxford University Press.

Silverman, W.K., LaGreca, A.M. and Wasserstein, S. (1995) 'What do children worry about? Worries and their relation to anxiety', *Child Development*, 66: 671–86.

Skinner, E.A. (1995) *Perceived Control, Motivation and Coping*. Thousand Oaks, CA: Sage.

Smith, P.K. and Levan, S. (1995) 'Perceptions and experiences of bullying in younger pupils', *British Journal of Educational Psychology*, 65: 489–500.

Smith, P.K. and Sharp, S. (eds) (1994) *School Bullying: Insights and Perspectives*. London: Routledge.

Smith, P.K. and Thompson, D. (1991) *Practical Approaches to Bullying*. London: David Fulton.

Smith, P.K., Cowie, H. and Sharp, S. (1994) 'Working directly with children in bullying situations', in P.K. Smith and S. Sharp (eds), *School Bullying: Insights and Perspectives*. London: Routledge.

Stacey, H. (1996) 'Mediation in the schools does go! An outline of the mediation process', *Pastoral Care in Education*, 14(2): 7–9.

Stephenson, P. and Smith, D. (1991) 'Why some schools don't have bullies', in M. Elliott (ed.), *Bullying: a Practical Guide to Coping for Schools*. Harlow: Longman.

Strasburger, V.C. (1995) *Adolescents and the Media: Medical and Psychological Impact*. Thousand Oaks, CA: Sage.

Takahashi, K. (1990) 'Are the key assumptions of the "Strange Situation" procedure universal? A view from Japanese research', *Human Development*, 33: 23–30.

Tattum, D. and Lane, D. (1989) *Bullying in Schools*. Stoke-on-Trent: Trentham Books.

Taylor, G. (1996) 'Circles of Friends', in H. Cowie and S. Sharp (eds), *Peer Counselling in Schools: a Time to Listen*. London: David Fulton.

Thompson, D.A. (1995) 'Two years on: problems in monitoring anti-bullying policies in schools and their effect on the incidence of bullying'. Paper presented at ECER conference, 14–15th September 1995, University of Bath, UK.

Trad, P.V. and Greenblatt, E. (1990) 'Psychological aspects of child stress: development and the spectrum of coping responses', in L. Eugene Arnold (ed.), *Childhood Stress*. New York: John Wiley.

Tuckman, B.W. (1965) 'Developmental sequence in small groups', *Psychological Bulletin*, 63: 384–99.

Turkel, S.B. and Eth, S. (1990) 'Psychopathological responses to stress: adjustment disorder and post-traumatic stress disorder in children and adolescents', in L. Eugene Arnold (ed.), *Childhood Stress*, New York: John Wiley.

United Nations (1991) *United Nations Convention on the Rights of the Child*. Innocenti Studies, Florence: UNICEF.

Valente, S.M., Saunders, S.J. and Street, R. (1988) 'Adolescent bereavement following suicide: an examination of relevant literature', *Journal of Counselling and Development*, 67: 174–7.

Wachtel, P.L. (1973) 'Psychodynamics, behaviour therapy and the implacable experimenter: an inquiry into the consistency of personality', *Journal of Abnormal Psychology*, 83: 324–34.

Warden, D. and Christie, D. (1997) *Teaching Social Behaviour*, London: David Fulton.

Watkins, C. (1995) *Behaviour Management*, Institute of Education School Improvement Network (Research Matters series).

Watson, J.B. and Raynor, R. (1920) 'Conditioned emotional reactions', *Journal of Experimental Psychology*, 3: 1–14.

Weisfeld, G. (1994) 'Aggression and dominance in the social world of boys', in John Archer (ed.), *Male Violence*. London: Routledge.

Weiss, R.S. (1991) 'The attachment bond in childhood and adulthood', in C.M. Parkes and J. Stevenson-Hinde (eds), *Attachment Across the Life Cycle*. London: Routledge.

Werner, E.E. (1989) 'High risk children in young adulthood: a longitudinal study from birth to age 32', *American Journal of Orthopsychiatry*, 59(1): 72–8.

Wetherington, E. and Kessler, R.C. (1991) 'Situations and processes of coping', in J. Eckenrode (ed.), *The Social Context of Coping*. New York: Plenum.

Wheldall, K., Morris, M., Vaughan, P. and Ng, Y.Y. (1981) 'Rows versus tables: an example of the use of behavioural ecology in two classes of 11 year old children', *Educational Psychology*, 1(2): 171–84.

Whitney, I. and Smith, P.K. (1993) 'A survey on the nature and extent of bully/victim problems in junior/middle and secondary schools', *Educational Research*, 35: 3–25.

Wilson, P. (1996) *Mental Health in Your School*. London: Jessica Kingsley.

Worden, J.W. (1991) *Grief Counselling and Grief Therapy*. London: Routledge.

Wright, J., Binney, V. and Smith, P.K. (1995) 'Security of attachment in 8- to 12-year-olds: a revised version of the Separation Anxiety Test, its psychometric properties and clinical interpretation', *Journal of Child Psychology and Psychiatry*, 36: 757–74.

Yamamoto, K., Suliman, A., Parsons, J. and Davies Jr., O.L. (1987) 'Voices in unison: stressful events in the lives of children in six countries', *Journal of Child Psychology and Psychiatry*, 28(6): 855–64.

Yule, W. and Williams, R. (1990) 'Post-traumatic stress reactions in children', *Journal of Traumatic Stress*, 3(2): 279–95.

Ziegler, S. and Rosenstein-Manner, M. (1991) *Bullying in School*. Toronto: Board of Education.

SUBJECT INDEX

NAME INDEX